BREAKTHROUGH:
WOMEN IN WRITING

BREAKTHROUGH:
Women in Writing

by Diana Gleasner

F82205

Walker and Company
New York

Library of Congress Cataloging in Publication Data

Gleasner, Diana C
  Women in Writing.

  (Breakthrough)
  Bibliography: p. 157
  SUMMARY: Describes the efforts of five women to
achieve success as authors. Emphasizes the particular
problems they faced in combining a writing career with
family responsibilities and in overcoming prejudice
against women writers.
  1. Women authors, American—Biography—Juvenile
literature. [1. Women authors, American.
2. Authors, American] I. Title. II. Series:
Breakthrough (New York)

PS151.G5   810'.9'9287 [B] [920]   79-6609
ISBN 0-8027-6384-7

First published in the United States of America in 1980
by the Walker Publishing Company, Inc.

Published simultaneously in Canada by Beaverbooks,
Limited, Pickering, Ontario.

ISBN: 0-8027-6384-7

Library of Congress Catalog Card Number: 79-6609

Printed in the United States of America

10 9 8 7 6 5 4 3 2 1

"Any woman who writes is a survivor"

Tillie Olsen

For my sister, Joanne Cottle Storch,
who understands

And for my writing friends
with love and thanks

CONTENTS

Acknowledgment

The author wishes to thank *Good Housekeeping* Magazine for use of quoted material from an article entitled "The Real Erma Bombeck" in its April, 1978, issue.

Introduction

IN KINDERGARTEN, we sat in a circle and told what we wanted to be. I said "a fireman," and everybody laughed. Instantly I understood my future would not be filled with action and heroism, so I laughed, too. At five, I knew I could not change the world, but I was determined to get along in it.

In high school, I was good at shooting baskets and throwing a football, but I soon realized that the same abilities that made a man more of a man made a woman less of a woman. My parents put a high premium on good grades and a college education but made it clear these preparations were to make me an educated mother, not a career woman. Writing seemed ideal. I could stay home, be a good mother, and still have a career.

When I purchased two copies of a magazine that had one of my first articles in it, my mother remarked that I had chosen an expensive hobby. When I made plans to go out of town to my first writer's conference, my father warned me not to leave my husband unattended. I went, anyway. If my marriage couldn't survive a week's absence, I reasoned, it wasn't worth saving.

Failure is easy for a married woman. She can announce she has lost interest in writing and let her husband support her. No one loses face. At first, I thought I was the only one who knew I was deeply serious about my career, but my husband bought me business cards, baby-sat while I attended writing workshops, and urged me to go all the way with it.

I need approval and plenty of love. I cannot overestimate the importance of his encouragement. He could not have guessed that years later my writing would support us (though hardly in the same style) while he served his apprenticeship as a photographer, just as he supported me while I struggled to launch myself as a writer.

At a conference of the Outdoor Writers Association of America, the editor of *Field and Stream* said his magazine might print an article by a woman if it was of an "introductory nature." "Expert" pieces would only be accepted from men. What was I doing in a field in which I could never aspire to write as an authority? I couldn't come up with the answer, so I switched to travel writing.

I am used to adapting. When a man congratulated me after I had endured a grueling marathon power-boat race by saying, "You're not a woman," I was able to translate it into the high compliment he intended. I wrote slanted articles for male editors because I wanted to be published and knew what they liked to hear from a woman. Confusing? Not at all. It was my world, and I had learned long before to cope without making a scene.

This is an honest book. The women's movement, which made it possible, has given me pride in my sex, which for years was a source of shame and frustration. I was not brave enough or strong enough (most of my fireman instincts having been squashed out of me) to be at the forefront of the movement. But I can follow with enthusiasm and gratitude.

What has impressed me, in working on this book, is how far we have come. I am also aware of how far we have to go. The story behind the injustices endured by women writers is the story of womankind. At one time, we were considered contaminated; we were later elevated to merely brainless. Amazingly, half the human race was simply written off as inferior. Women were denied freedom, education, the right to vote, to own property, and to live an active life. The wonder is that they could raise a voice at all.

In spite of great progress, the idea that a woman take up writing as a serious business is still being questioned. In the eighteenth century, Fanny Burney had her brother submit her novel to their father's publisher, who printed it anonymously. Nineteenth-century writers Mary Ann Evans and Lucille Dupin hid their sex behind the now-famous names George Eliot and George Sand. In this century, a male critic, who had evidently forgotten about menstruation and babies, thundered that women can't be writers because they don't know anything about blood and guts. He was not questioned. After all, he was speaking confidently out of a strong tradition against women in literature.

Those first women who dared to write for publication were members of the upper class who had access to learning. It wasn't easy. Timidity was as much a part of them as the marrow of their bones, and publishing power belonged exclusively to men. If they had written angrily or even boldly, we wouldn't have their words today.

In the seventeenth century, the Duchess of Newcastle, convinced that as a female she was working with an inadequate brain, wrote a great deal on the inferiority of women. Countess Anne Finch (born in 1661) may have agreed that women were basically featherbrained, but she was smart enough to publish her first volume of poems anonymously. She knew her writing would meet with "prejudice if not contempt" and that a "woman that attempts the pen" is "an intruder on the rights of men."

The first known English woman to write professionally, that is for money, was Aphra Behn (1640-1698). Critics called her "that lewd harlot," although she was a talented playwright, novelist, and poet. Bravely, she demanded to be judged by her work, not her sex. Unfortunately, she was ahead of her time. Many years would pass before writing would be considered a proper activity for a woman.

Some promising, although isolated, advances were made in the eighteenth century. After a shaky beginning, Fanny Burney's writing established her as the first important woman novelist in England. She burned her early work when her stepmother declared writing "unsuitable" for a girl. While copying her father's *History of Music* by hand, she secretly wrote *Evelina-or a Young Lady's Entrance into the World.* It was published anonymously, the author referred to as a man "well versed in the manners of the times."

Mary Wollstonecraft, the most noted feminist of her time, wrote fiction and nonfiction opposing the oppression of women. She knew her subject well. Her alcoholic father had been brutal, and she saw her sister trapped in a miserable marriage. Her *Vindication of the Rights of Women* (1792) was an intelligent, passionate appeal for women's independence. One of her frustrations was that publishers allowed male characters to be portrayed in full dimension, yet women had to be melded "into one character of yielding softness and gentle compliance." One of her fictional characters sums up the problem: "Was not the world a vast prison and women born slaves?"

Of the women who wrote before the 1800s, few are known today, but as more females were exposed to education, they erupted into print in greater numbers. Hostility and ridicule were too high a price for all but the bravest. It was up to the nineteenth-century writers to rise above the traditional thinking that refused to take a woman or her work seriously.

In 1810, Mary Brunton wrote anonymously rather than be, in her words, "abhorred as literary women are." She would prefer, she said, to "exhibit as a rope dancer." Some tried to avoid trouble by using masculine pen names. In 1849, Charlotte Brontë, who used the pen name 'Currer Bell,' wrote, "I wish you did not think me a woman. I wish all my reviewers believed Currer Bell to be a man; they would be more just to him."

Some women adopted the role of helpless femininity. Mrs. Oliphant asked an editor of a masculine magazine whether "a womanish story-teller like myself may not become wearisome." Most women believed in their own inferiority, but it did not silence them. Jane Austen produced memorable books, though she had to hide her writing under her needlework.

Women were making progress despite strong prejudice against education and careers for females. Victorian physicians and anthropologists thought women's inferiority was due to smaller and less efficient brains like the "lower races." As a result, even upper-class women stayed home doing housework while their brothers went away to the university. Those with a natural talent for writing tried to educate themselves. This annoyed men like G. H. Lewes, who complained in 1847 that the literary profession was being invaded by "women, children and ill-trained troops." A character in Jane Austen's *Persuasion* said that a woman who has the misfortune of knowing something "should conceal it as well as she can."

Women were torn by an internal tug of war. The definition of a woman was in conflict with the definition of a writer. Poet laureate Robert Southey summed up the attitude of the age in a letter (1837) to Charlotte Brontë. "Literature cannot be the business of a woman's life and it ought not to be." Her father told her the same thing. She replied that she was trying to give up reading and writing because her father's approval meant so much to her.

Approval! What female (or male!) has ever escaped the need for it? Certainly not the Victorians. The model woman then was defined as absolutely pure and utterly self-sacrificing, a perfect wife and mother. Beauty and domesticity, assets that would help women marry and raise a family, were all that mattered. Above all else, women were conditioned to be economically and emotionally dependent. They balanced precariously on the tightrope between their need for approval and their need to explore their potential.

Many people thought only frustrated women wrote. Charlotte Brontë's publisher believed she would have given up "all her genius and all her fame to have been beautiful." Those who tried to be happy homemakers and writers, too, found the going tough. No wonder the enduring contributions of the last century and a half were mainly made by unmarried women: Jane Austen, Emily Brontë, Christina Rossetti, Emily Dickinson, and Louisa May Alcott, and by George Eliot, Elizabeth Barrett Browning, and Charlotte Brontë, who married in their thirties. Those few writers who married, had children, and produced lasting work were blessed with servants.

Even worse than the pressures of society against writing was the widely held belief that women were inferior. As second-class citizens, they lacked confidence in their own experience. And, of course, they knew that their literature was, by definition, minor.

Women who managed to buck the tide of the times and see their work published were rewarded with a double standard of criticism. Some who used male pen names found their books reviewed a second time when their true identity was learned. All sorts of new criticism came to light. George Eliot was suddenly criticized by reviewers who thought it wrong for a woman "to lay so much stress on the bodily feelings of the other sex."

Charlotte Brontë bristled at being judged because she was a woman. She told a critic of the *Economist*, "To you I am neither man nor woman. I come before you as an author only. It is the sole standard by which you have a right to judge me—the sole ground on which I accept your judgment."

In spite of all the unfair treatment, more and more women turned to writing. They had no say in the institutions that ruled them, the government or the church. Writing provided an avenue for expression, a chance for change.

In the twentieth century, doors opened for women that had been previously bolted shut. They gained the right to vote, own property, and achieve a higher education. Birth control offered a choice, and a longer lifespan gave them time. Technology eased domestic chores. Experiences were open to them that had previously been denied. The result? Many more women wrote with greatly increased productivity.

The problems of the woman writer did not evaporate. In a 1931 essay, Virginia Woolf spoke of self-censorship, saying she wanted to "speak the truth about her passions" but then remembered what men would say. The writer in her was silenced. Katherine Anne Porter complained that her female upbringing made her feel she was expected to give service to anyone who demanded it. Shortly before taking her own life, Sylvia Plath said, "A woman has to sacrifice all claims to femininity and family to be a writer."

Women have been thoroughly programmed by a culture that treats females as essentially inferior. They are

considered passive, dependent, seductive, overly emotional, and nurturing creatures regardless of their individual
characteristics. This conditioning process has to be experienced to fully understand its impact. It begins at
birth and is reinforced daily until we die.

It is ironic that language, which reflects the attitudes of
our society, has been used against us. The only tools a
writer has to work with are words. Yet we don't need to be
told that bachelor and spinster are not equal terms, that
men who call women "chicks" do not hold them in high
esteem. "Barefoot and pregnant" is only a joke, we are
assured. Some say it's silly to try to change our language.
Had I been a smarter five-year-old, I would have
understood that the word "fireman" made it off limits
from the start. No one has to tell us that the status and
power is on the side of a major, not a majorette, a gover-
nor, not a governess, a poet, not a poetess.

We have been taught to seek approval by being feminine, but my dictionary defines feminine as "like a
woman, weak, gentle," which doesn't sound exactly like a
winner. Aggressiveness and bravery are considered
masculine characteristics. Our children's books used to
picture boys having adventures, girls staying home and
sweeping the kitchen. I remember one vividly that showed
a boy sitting at a big desk with the presidential seal of the
United States of America behind him while his sister
pushed a baby carriage with a *kitten* in it. On television
ads, men win races and women suffer with embarrass-
ment because their husband's collar is dirty. Our history
books, mostly written by men, have left out or down-
played the contributions of women. Our encyclopedias
have referred to the "pioneer and his wife." Was not the
nameless wife a pioneer, also?

Girls' sports in high school were a joke. Competition
was not feminine, so we had no interscholastic games. We
had play days and served each other refreshments. Win-

ning, we were told, was not important. In college, we were encouraged to pick out silver patterns, while the men planned their careers. We didn't know *any* women who were doctors or lawyers or politicians. The rare ones who made their own living were considered a little strange and were pitied for their failure to get a man. We were someone's daughter, someone's wife, someone's mother. Somewhere along the way, we lost our identities.

Voices were raised in protest, at first just a few, then many. Women began to reject their image as second class. They insisted on being heard. H. H. Richardson, on being told to give up writing and have babies, declared, "There are enough women to do the child bearing and child rearing. I know of none who can write my books." Sylvia Ashton-Warner declared, "I don't mean to go down under marriage and babies . . . never to be heard of again." Kate Brown, a character in Doris Lessing's *The Summer Before the Dark,* said, "The light that is the desire to please has gone out. And about time, too."

Then, in 1963, along came Betty Friedan, who expressed the female dilemma in her best-selling book *The Feminine Mystique.* She challenged the idea that women, no matter how gifted or intelligent, should give up all interest in the affairs of the world and devote their lives solely to husbands and children. The book proved to be a major turning point, and in its wake other feminist books followed: Caroline Bird's *Born Female* (1968), Kate Millet's *Sexual Politics* (1969), and Germaine Greer's *The Female Eunuch* (1970). At first, female activists were called "libbers" and were jeered at by the press. Gradually, the women's movement gained momentum and was recognized as a powerful force that wasn't going to go away.

Women began to discover their anger and to get in touch with their long-repressed sexuality. At last, they could be honest with themselves and their readers. More doors were opened for women in the 1960s, and they flew through them with a rich outpouring of creativity. Their contributions changed literature. Fresh territory was being discovered. "Something new is happening," said James H. Silberman, editor in chief of Random House. "Women are reinterpreting experience."

We began to realize that we couldn't really be free, effective, independent adults unless we were able to support ourselves. Although advances had been made since 1872, when it was literally a crime to vote, we still were denied equal pay for equal work, equal employment opportunities, equal education, equal political representation, and equal treatment under the law.

The economic outlook for women writers has improved dramatically in the last ten years. Because they are finally able to write honest books, because there is a large readership awaiting those books, and because they are able to take themselves and their work seriously, some have been able to command large advance payments for their writing. Successful books by female authors are sought by reprint houses and film producers. Publishers who understand profit have come to respect the power of the female pen.

The flip side of this rosy scenario is that there is plenty of prejudice still around. My editor's juvenile biography of the Wright Brothers was turned down in the sixties by one publisher who said a book about airplanes should be written by a man. We still have reviewers with preconditioned attitudes. A male critic recently referred to the "domestic imagery" in Margaret Atwood's poetry, although seven-eighths of the poems take place outdoors. We live in a society in which women have a powerfully ingrained fear that success is defeminizing. "She writes like a man" is still considered a compliment.

No one has come up with the final answer to the home/mother/career conflict. A woman writer at home is considered a housewife. A man at home is a writer who must not be disturbed. Women with relatives, friends, acquaintances, husbands, and/or children are interruptible. They have been raised to be available. Deciding not to dust is one thing, a crying child quite another.

How do we handle the double demands and the pervasive guilt? With considerable difficulty. After interviewing Erica Jong, I called home to find the orthodontist had tried unsuccessfully to reach us because our daughter was so traumatized by her new braces. My rationale—that our teenagers would develop character during our short absences—disintegrated. Surely, Steve was fine, sixteen, and blessed with straight teeth. The answer—"Steve's moaning on the bathroom floor"—did not fall into the reassuring category. The combination of fasting to make weight for a wrestling match and running six miles had not agreed with him. My careful stocking of the refrigerator was for naught. My son would starve in my absence. Who did I think I was, trying to swing a career and a family? I understood Erica Jong's statement "Guilt is my constant companion."

We called our North Carolina home from Santa Fe, New Mexico, after interviewing Judy Blume. At 11 P.M., we got a recorded message. "Dear Mom and Dad," a shaky voice said, "The police are searching for an armed murderer in the area. Sue and I are staying with neighbors." What kind of a mother was I? I had never thought to leave instructions for a murderer-loose-in-the-neighborhood situation. I knew at some deep protoplasmic level what Judy Blume meant when she spoke of the conflicts of work and family.

I did not mind that my interview with Erica Jong was interrupted so she could nurse her baby. I had left the oral defense of my thesis for my M.A. degree for the same reason.

It seemed entirely normal that my interview with Judy

Blume was interrupted by (1) the Roto Rooter man, (2) the plumber, (3) the Roto Rooter man again (with the disappointing news that the situation was hopeless), (4) her son having lost her gasoline credit card, (5) putting the roast in, (6) her husband home early to shop for snacks for an evening meeting, (7) giving her daughter instructions for dinner preparations so we wouldn't be interrupted.

When I ask a stranger at a cocktail party what he does for a living, he often returns the courtesy by asking what my husband does. Once I answered, "He's a photographer and I'm a writer," only to be asked if I wrote captions for his pictures. I said I sometimes did. It's true. I sometimes do. But of course it's only a fragment of a truth, enough perhaps for a martini-shortened attention span.

Not all women give in so easily. In 1975, Adrienne Rich refused the Pulitzer Prize for poetry in her own name, accepting it instead in the name of the women whose voices "still go unheard in a patriarchal world, and in the name of those who, like us, have been tolerated as token women in this culture, often at great cost and in great pain . . . the silent women whose voices have been denied us, the articulate women who have given us strength to do our work."

We are shackled yet, but some of the hack marks are almost all the way through. Today we have women writers setting courageous examples, women whose lives are a study in the ability to endure. Writers are sharing their lives with enlightened men who have joined in the struggle for human liberation. We now read full-blooded stories based on female experience that defy literary conventions of the past. Women on all sides are soaring toward new galaxies on wings of the printed word.

They offer sound advice: novelist Toni Morrison urging us to break out of the mold men have made for us, to "be adventuresome, courageous, be willing to think the un-thinkable"; Virginia Woolf reminding us that "literature is no one's private ground; literature is common ground. Let us trespass freely and fearlessly and find our way for ourselves."

Let us get on with our work.

Judy Blume

Sobbing, Judy Blume hauled her heavy electric typewriter to the edge of the canyon behind her New Mexico home. "I'm through," she said to herself. "I'll never write again." Trembling with effort, the 101-pound woman lifted the machine as high as she could. She wanted to do a thorough job of finishing off her career.

Judy Blume, author of eleven best-selling books for children, had once thought she would be satisfied forever if only someone would publish one of her stories. She had not dared dream of reaching millions of readers or seeing her work adapted for television. Her wishes had been simple. "Oh, please," she whispered as she mailed her manuscripts. "Somebody publish me."

Without her typewriter, she would no longer be able to write. No more books meant no more vicious reviews. Why were reviewers so heartless? Weren't they human? Her readers were human, shy boys confused by the adult world, vulnerable young girls who shared their secrets with her. Letters from readers provided some of the most satisfying moments of her career. Suddenly, she realized she would not be able to answer the stacks of fan mail on her desk without her typewriter. Slowly, she let it down to rest on her knees. The bottom of the canyon dissolved behind a fresh flow of tears. *Maybe I'll need this machine,* she thought as she lugged the typewriter back toward the house.

15

On the verge of giving up a career that was the envy of
writers everywhere, she recalled the tremendous effort she
had put into getting published more than a dozen years
before. As a young New Jersey housewife, she had studied
hundreds and hundreds of library books, dividing them
into two groups. Group-one books were boring. Group
two were fun, books she read to her childen, books she
wished she had written. Then, imitating the style of some
of her favorites, Judy tried to write her own.

The decision to try had been an important one. She
had been raised to be a housewife and mother, but at the
age of twenty-seven, it was simply not enough. The suburban scene was comfortable; there was plenty of money.
But where were the outlets for her creativity? Where were
the challenges? She was struggling with the suffocating
feeling that every exciting thing that was going to happen
to her had already happened.

Her first manuscript, lovingly composed and carefully
typed, was mailed with high hopes. How beautifully it
had rhymed. As she waited for the publisher's response,
daydreams flickered in the back of her mind. They'll take
it, she dared to hope, and it will be a great success. Other
times, priding herself on her realistic approach to life, she
thought, *So what if they don't publish my story.*

The printed rejection slip attached to her returned
story demolished both states of mind. She hid in the closet
so her kids wouldn't see her cry. There, muffled by coats,
she let go of her "so what" approach. She was frustrated,
angry, hurt. Why couldn't they see the value of her work?
In the morning, she woke with fresh resolve. She would
redouble her efforts.

Judy wrote more books, picture books for prekindergar-
ten children like her own. As her productivity increased,
so did the rejections, but now she was getting used to
them. They were discouraging but not devastating. She

sent her stories out over and over, never changing them, always hoping the next publisher would rush one into publication. Some of the rejection slips were clearly dead ends; the others were worded so that they seemed to her to hold out a glimmer of encouragement. "And I desperately needed encouragement," she said. "I felt so isolated. I didn't know anyone who was writing."

When Judy heard New York University was offering a course in juvenile writing, she signed up immediately. It was a decision she never regretted. Monday night became the highlight of her week. She would take the train from her New Jersey home into the city and have supper alone in a restaurant before class. "For the first time in my life, I felt really independent," she said. "And the people there understood what I was trying to do. We shared our dreams and our discouragements and even began to unravel some of the mysteries of the publishing world."

As the course drew to a conclusion, she couldn't stand the thought of being without it, so she took it again. Although she didn't sell any books while enrolled in the class, she did sell several short children's stories to religious magazines. Very little money was involved, but the encouragement was worth more than money to her. She set to work furiously turning out stories. What a great satisfaction it was to see "Iggie's House," her tale of a black family that moved into an all-white neighborhood, serialized in a magazine. Still, she held on to the dream of seeing her work between the hard covers of a genuine book.

Two and a half years went by; twenty children's books had been submitted, and a shoe box held the rewards of her efforts—a pile of rejection slips. The realities of the marketplace for fiction were grim, but she was learning. If six rejection slips landed in her mailbox in one week, well, she was working on six new projects.

As a mother of two small children, Judy worked around a schedule in which interruptions were the norm, and quiet blocks of time so fragile they were unnerving. When the ring of the phone took her from the typewriter for the fourth time in one day, she sighed. Writers of juvenile fiction, she decided, should be childless or at least phoneless. An editor with Reilly and Lee was calling to tell her they thought "The One in the Middle is the Green Kangaroo" would make an attractive book. Judy Blume hung up in disbelief. A book! She ran downstairs to where her children and their friends were playing. She threw clay around the kitchen shouting with joy until one frightened little boy ran home with the news that "Mrs. Blume has gone crazy." Later that week, the mailman, who had brought so many discouraging Manila envelopes to the Blume residence, delivered a slim envelope containing a $350 advance. "Hey, do you know what this means!" she shrieked, grabbing him by the sleeve. They danced across the front lawn while she gave him a garbled version of her dream coming true.

Sobbing in the closet and dancing across the lawn are brief moments in a writing career. Mostly, Judy learned that nothing happens without a good deal of self-discipline translated into many hours at the typewriter. At least, she thought, her efforts would be taken more seriously now that she was a published author. She was thoroughly fed up with her husband's jokes about her work. "All I have to do," he would announce to their friends at parties, "is buy Judy some paper and pencils and she's happy. Isn't it wonderful! It keeps her out of Saks." He didn't try to stop her. She sometimes felt he didn't really care very much what she did as long as it didn't interfere with his life, but to have her work dismissed as a joke, that hurt!

Jubilant with success, Judy plunged ahead with a new

book idea. She also mailed out her previously rejected manuscripts, along with the magazine serialization of "Iggie's House." She had read in *Writer's Digest* magazine that Bradbury Press was interested in realistic fiction for young people. Rather than a rejection or an acceptance, Bradbury sent her a letter asking her to meet with them in New York.

Mailing off manuscripts to editors was one thing, meeting them in person quite another. Judy dressed carefully, eager to make a good impression. As eagerness dissolved into terror, her stomach knotted painfully. She took a pill to quiet her nerves, but it left her mouth so dry she could hardly talk. Luckily, Dick Jackson turned out to be not only a perceptive editor but also a sensitive human being who put her immediately at ease. They were interested in "Iggie's House" but not in its present form. He asked hundreds of questions about the characters, the plot, and the general direction of the book while Judy scribbled voluminous notes to herself. No contract was offered, but Jackson said if she could do a successful rewrite, Bradbury Press was interested in working with her. "I labored over that book for a month," she remembers. "Finally, when I had done all I could do, I sent it back to them. They called with the great news that they were accepting the book for publication."

Those first two books are ones Judy would like to forget. "They aren't very good," she says. "They were imitations of books I'd admired, but I learned something from them. The most important lesson was that until you pull it out of your own heart, it doesn't really work."

Now that she had accomplished the goal of seeing her work published, Judy wanted to try a different writing style. She decided to write a novel for adolescents, the kind of book she would have loved to read when she was twelve or thirteen. She pushed publishing taboos out of her mind and wrote what sixth grade was like for her. The story poured out, and the first draft was completed in six short weeks. Writing for twelve-year-olds had a lot of appeal. "When you're that age," she says, "everything is still out there in front of you. You have the opportunity to be almost anyone you want. I was not yet thirty when I started the book, but I felt my options were already gone."

Are You There, God, It's Me Margaret was the story of a young girl struggling simultaneously with such momentous concerns as religion and menstruation. This was one children's book that was written from the gut. Margaret's thoughts and feelings had been Judy's when she was twelve. She prepared herself for rejection, knowing she was dealing with sensitive subject matter. At least, she consoled herself, she had written an honest book. But Bradbury was delighted with the freshness of the story, and it went on to become a juvenile best seller.

When the *New York Times* published a laudatory review of the book, Judy experienced one of the highest points of her career. People were actually taking her work seriously. *My God,* she thought, *even though I know I don't know how to write, the* New York Times *thinks I do.* She sang in the car and hummed all the way through the grocery store.

Margaret reached a large receptive audience. The mail, which started within a year of the book's publication in 1971, has never stopped. "She knows just how I feel," said one thirteen-year-old. "It's like she's still a kid." A twelve-year-old girl wrote, "You don't know what a comfort it is to read about kids your own age through these troublesome years." Over and over readers tell her, "You are writing about me. I feel like you know all my secrets."

When asked for some Blume titles, one bookseller just

laughed and pointed to an empty shelf. "That's where they're supposed to be. I can't keep them in stock." Getting a Judy Blume book out of the library often involves a long wait. But it is the outpouring of letters—thousands and thousands of them—that is most gratifying to the author.

"I have a wonderful, intimate relationship with kids," she says. "My books seem to make them feel a little less alone in the world. I would like to have found that satisfaction in the books I was reading when I was young. I never knew there were other kids thinking what I was thinking or feeling the same things sexually."

Her success in reaching adolescents comes from her honest treatment of the concerns that involve them the most deeply. "I think I write about sexuality," she explains, "because when I was young, that's what I most wanted to know about. I identify very strongly with kids. Twelve- and thirteen-year-olds feel things very intensely. They need to know about what they are feeling, and more than anything else, they want reassurance that their feelings are normal. Besides, sex is very interesting."

Judy is able to write convincingly because she is blessed with almost total recall. "That's my talent if there is a talent involved," she says. Since she can remember details so vividly (like what she was wearing the day another kindergartener stepped on her finger and made her cry in front of the whole class), it's easy to project herself back to certain stages in her life. "I tell a story by putting myself into the main character's shoes and asking how would I feel—what would I do—if this happened to me."

"I write out of my own needs as a child," she explains. "I read Nancy Drew mysteries and biographies and books about girls whose main problem was that they wanted a horse, but I didn't find any satisfaction in them. I turned to adult books early, but they weren't satisfying, either. I wanted to read about myself, and so that's what I try to give kids — a look at themselves, their desires, fears, and uncertainties."

"My responsibility to be honest with my readers is my strongest motivation," she says. "I am offended by dishonest books. I hate the idea that you should always protect children. They live in the same world we do. They see and hear things. Secrets are terrible because what they imagine and have to deal with alone is usually scarier than the truth."

After *Margaret,* Judy tackled other sensitive issues with the same frank approach. *Then Again Maybe I Won't* dealt with shoplifting and wet dreams from a boy's point of view. *It's Not the End of the World* explored an adolescent's adjustment to her parents' divorce. *Tales of a Fourth Grade Nothing* was a story of sibling rivalry. Following quickly one after another came *Deenie* (dealing with the dual problems of a physical disability and a parent living vicariously through her children), *Blubber* (children's cruelty toward each other), and *Otherwise Known as Sheila the Great* (hidden fears). *Forever* was by far the most controversial of the Blume books and *Starring Sally J. Freedman as Herself* the most autobiographical.

Within the space of a few short years, Judy Blume had created a revolution in the world of children's books, become a hero to countless adolescents, and seeded the clouds of controversy until she stood dead center in the middle of the resulting storm.

When *Margaret* was published, Judy proudly took three copies to her children's school library. When she asked her daughter if any of her friends were reading the book, Randy said they weren't in the library. Judy investigated and found that the male principal wouldn't allow them in the school because they dealt with menstruation.

Then came the news that school libraries in Richmond, Virginia; Tulsa, Oklahoma; Lenox, Massachusetts; and a host of other cities banned some of her books. Parents were objecting to the frank language and mature themes. The word from England was "There are no proper story lines and no proper endings for British children."

Those who rushed to shield their children from the "evils" of Margaret became catatonic at the idea of *Forever*. At the request of her daughter, who was then thirteen, Judy wrote the story of teenagers, both good students from loving families, who fall in love. They make a vow that their love will last forever, and eventually they have intercourse. Their parting is sad but without the added trauma of abortion, venereal disease, pregnancy, or even the hint of a nervous breakdown.

Dell refused to publish a paperback edition of *Forever* because they were afraid Blume's loyal fifth- and sixth-grade readers would automatically reach for any book with her name on it. A deluge of letters arrived shortly after its publication from indignant parents and librarians who had purchased the book without knowing its contents. Many feared the story would give kids "ideas" before they were ready for them, that it raised problems without solving them.

Judy is the first to admit she doesn't have solutions. Her purpose is to get problems out in the open where they can be discussed. Whether or not parents will permit this kind of discussion depends, says Judy, on "whether they feel that what was good enough for them is good enough for their kids."

As for her own childhood, Judy describes herself as two people. The outside Judy was a very good girl. She brought home A's from school, belonged to a Girl Scout troop, and almost never disobeyed her parents. Pleasing them was very important to her. "My brother came first,

Judy at about age four

and he did everything wrong, so I knew I had to do everything right."

"We never talked about problems in our family," she remembers. "My father explained where babies came from, but I never dared ask about how my body could feel. It would have been such a relief to me if I could have read *Deenie* when I was twelve. Then I would have known that other kids masturbated. I kept making deals with God. I would only do it twice a week if He would make sure this or that happened."

Judy at left, age thirteen, with best friend at Camp Kenwood

The "inside" Judy had an exciting and sometimes wicked fantasy life. She and her friends giggled over the "dirty" parts of adult books. The forbidden secrets of the grown-up world loomed beyond her grasp, but her imagination was concocting some interesting answers to the many questions stirring in her brain.

No one suspected what was going on inside Judy's head. They only knew she was an easy child to entertain. "You can give Judy an old pair of shoes and she will play all day," her mother would say. Her dolls were characters with complex personalities created in much the same ways she would later make up characters for her books.

Not all Judy's energies were put into private imaginings. She was actually impatiently waiting to be "discovered," whereupon her career as an actress would bloom and flourish to much public acclaim. "I was very 'show biz'," she remembers. "When I was ten and lived in Florida, I staged a ballet complete with costumes for the entire apartment house. I was director, choreographer and star. I also made the programs. After "Starring . . . ," I inserted my name until someone talked me out of it. However, she adds with a sparkle, "I did manage to give myself a solo."

While growing up was scary, it was exciting. There were no limits on her horizons. She could be, would be, anything she wanted. Her mother played the traditional housewife role, but her father, Rudolf Sussman, a dentist, did an awful lot of parenting. "It was my father who cut my toenails, took my temperature, and shampooed my hair when I had some kind of dreadful impetigo. He sat in the bathroom with me while I had stomach cramps. I spent a lot of time down in his shop in the basement. He was very important to me."

Looking back, Judy sees that her mother, Esther Sussman, should have had a career, "but in those days it wasn't acceptable." In her opinion, it would have been better for the whole family if she had, as her mother has many talents and is a highly organized woman.

Judy's school experiences were very positive. "I grew up in Elizabeth, which had the only all-girls public high school in the whole state of New Jersey. There weren't any boys, so we did everything. We ran the sports, the newspaper, the yearbook—so I never knew the feeling of discrimination. In fact, while I was in school there wasn't anything that I felt I couldn't do because I was a girl. But

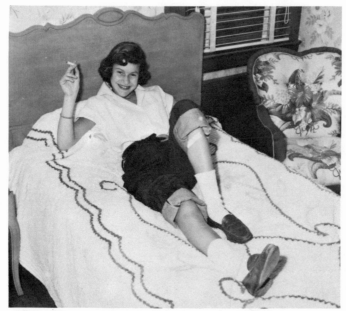

Judy at fifteen, trying to look sophisticated. She has never smoked.

I went to college to be a teacher because I was influenced by my mother's practical wishes for me. I knew my goal in college was to meet a man and get married. I wanted a degree in case I ever had to work, but I wasn't really thinking. I was very busy wanting to get married and have babies and play grownup."

Judy's career as a student at Boston University was short-lived. After orientation week, college officials called Judy's parents with the news that she was very sick. "That was the beginning of all my troubles with illness," she recalls. "I had mononucleosis and had to be carried off the plane in a stretcher. It was very frightening." When she was well enough to attend school again, she chose New York University so she could be near her doctor. Various physical problems continued to plague her, especially at exam time when she developed excruciating

Judy at sixteen

stomach pains. "Now I'm convinced that many of my problems were caused by emotions," she says. "It bothers me that no doctor was ever wise enough to suggest that maybe some psychiatric help was needed. I would not let myself think about it because psychiatry was a very dirty word in my family. Why would my parents' 'perfect' daughter need a psychiatrist? Oh, I was so busy being perfect."

When she was a sophomore at New York University, Judy fell in love with John Blume, who, at twenty-seven, was already an established lawyer. Judy was twenty-one and about to get married when her wonderful father died suddenly. After that, she realized life was a fragile affair and that she had better make every day count.

She married Blume during her junior year but waited until after she graduated to have her first child. Daughter Randy was followed two years later by Larry, and Judy settled down to full-time motherhood. The idea of marriage, which had once been so exciting, turned out to be far less exciting in reality. Nevertheless, she was determined to make the best of it. Gradually, she realized all her options were gone. "My father always encouraged me to get out there and catch the moon. But after a few years I began to think, *Well, kid, this is where it's at for you. He does whatever he wants, and you stay home and do all these dirty jobs.* As a child, I had missed the traditional female brainwashing. Maybe that's why I was so resentful later on."

The lines from *Wifey*, Judy's adult novel, seem to fit. "Is this it, then? Is this what my life is all about? Driving the kids to and from school and decorating our final house? Oh, mother, dammit! Why did you bring me up to think THIS was what I wanted? And now that I know it's not, what am I supposed to do about it?"

What Judy tried to do was adjust. She would outline in her head the good things about her situation. There was enough money, she enjoyed her children, and she had a certain amount of freedom. She would shrug and think, *So what if I'm not happy.*

Judy is convinced that terrible things happen to an imaginative child who finds no outlet for her creativity as an adult. The terrible things for her were illness, fevers, rashes, allergies and a general state of depression. "I was raised for marriage and motherhood, but it wasn't enough. I needed something of my own."

She gave up trying to write popular songs when she realized they weren't really good and she didn't know how to go about selling them. Judy had an artistic flair and had always liked working with her hands. The large felt pictures she designed for her children's rooms drew praise from everyone who saw them, so she decided to go into business making them. Her first sales mission to Bloomingdale's was successful. She glued the colorful banners together for a year in her cellar "sweat shop" until she became allergic to the glue.

When she was reading to her three- and five-year-olds, she thought some of the books she took out of the library weren't very good. "I could do better than this," she said to herself. After her course in juvenile writing and an extended apprenticeship of trial-and-error learning, Judy proved that she could indeed write children's books as well as realistic fiction for adolescents. Success brought new challenges, new ideas, new people. Her life wasn't dead-ended, after all. Now she had something of her own, a career, along with another surprising bonus — impressive earning power.

She had found a way to be independent. Had she not achieved success as a writer, she doubts she would ever have dared to think about a divorce. When she finally did take the first step to dissolve her marriage, her friends said, "Oh, God, you're so lucky. You have a way of getting out." Two years after she wrote *It's Not the End of the World,* about a young girl who learns to cope with her parents' divorce, Judy's divorce became official.

In 1975, Judy took her children with her when she flew to Oklahoma to receive a book award. That was one flight none of them would ever forget. They all had a hilarious time with a bearded man sitting across from them on the

Judy in 1966 with Randy and Larry

plane. First impressions were misleading. Tom Kitchens thought Judy was the children's older sister, the children thought Tom was a kid, and Judy thought he was probably a ski bum. Tom turned out to be a physicist working for the National Science Foundation in Washington, D.C.

Tom and Judy's friendship developed as they mailed notes back and forth until finally she invited him to New Jersey to help chaperone Randy's party. She tried to sort out her feelings, questioning whether she liked Tom as much as she thought she did or if she was just terribly lonely. When Tom's job required a transfer, she knew the answer. Judy, Randy, and Larry followed Tom to London, England. There had been a time not long before when she thought she would never again consider being "someone's wife." The idea of marrying brought on her allergies, but she couldn't imagine a future without him. In May 1976, Tom and Judy exchanged their marriage vows.

When Tom was transferred, this time to New Mexico to head a materials research group at the atomic laboratory, Judy again packed up her children and typewriter. The family looked forward to skiing in the mountains, and Judy was excited by the challenge of writing for the first time for adults. The story had been developing in her head for a long time, so the characters were beginning to feel like old friends. Santa Fe, New Mexico, was a cosmopolitan town full of interesting, creative people who were used to celebrities. "This town is like nowhere else on earth," Judy says. "Celebrities come here because people are too blasé to bother them. The town's full of them." Since stories about her phenomenal success as an author had begun to appear in national magazines, that was an important consideration.

Bothered by the conflicting demands of career, wife, and motherhood, Judy decided to rent a small office. It sounded good. *The children will go to school,* she thought. *Tom will go to work, and I will go to my office.* It didn't work. "Oh, it did help me get started on *Wifey,* but we had just moved, and when a family is in that kind of transition period, someone has to help get it all together. That usually falls on a mom. In spite of the office, I was still responsible for meals and the grocery shopping and running the household. Even though I removed myself from it a few hours a day, it was there waiting for me."

"Occasionally," she admits, "I really let off steam about it. 'God dammit,' I'd yell, 'I'm spending my whole day grocery shopping and cooking. I'm not a cook. I'm supposed to be in there writing. Remember that's what I do for a living. That's my WORK.' Then I'd think, this is

Randy's last year at home before she goes to college, and we're having a nice time together. So what if I don't work every minute."

Book-promoting tours worked a special hardship on her. "For a long stretch, I was gone every week and home for the weekend. If someone had been sick in my absence, I just felt terrible. It wasn't smooth. We had just moved and were living out of cartons. We were all trying to adjust to new schools, new people, and a new town. I had hired someone to cook in my absence so the burden wouldn't fall on Randy's shoulders, but the family soon tired of that arrangement. I would arrive Friday night, absolutely exhausted, and my son would say, only half in jest, 'You look familiar. What's your name again?' "

"All I wanted to do was go to bed for the whole weekend, and yet I felt I had to be everything to everyone. In two days, I had to cook, be a wonderful mother, see a soccer game, be a great lover, and go out in the evening with Tom so he had some sort of social life. It was very tough. Men don't go through this. How easily they can say, 'I have a business trip'; they pack and they go. Part of this has got to be our fault as women for allowing ourselves to feel that we have to handle everything. The guilt tears you apart. Sometimes when I get really upset and scream that I'm not able to work because I have all of this other stuff to do, Tom says, 'Whose fault is that? Just forget it and go to work.' But it's not that easy."

"I don't know the answer for my generation," Judy says thoughtfully. "I think that for our children it's going to be different. I know Randy's growing up feeling without question that she will have work. And her work will be as important as her mate's work, if she chooses to have a mate. Young men seem to understand that more and more. But there are still a lot of the old values around. I originally saw my role as being a perfect wife and mother.

Neither my mother nor myself ever questioned the way of life where the man is king. I still have not answered some of the conflicts in myself. How does one do all this? Instead of being resentful, I've decided to enjoy these last few years my children are at home."

Judy wishes the women's movement had gathered momentum earlier in her life. "What I see for my daughter are all the options open to her. She can decide exactly what she wants of life. But I'm still not sure that we're ever going to solve, in my lifetime, anyway, the woman/mother/career question because women are still going to have the babies. Then what? Someone has to care for the baby. Some of my younger friends are having one child later, after they have established a career. Then they take a short leave of absence and hire someone to care for the child when they return to work. They seem to be able to pull it off, which I think is wonderful. I think that type of independence is very important. Those of us who went from mommy and daddy to husband have never known that." Yet she admits she likes having kids grown up while she's still a young forty. "I look at the kids, the ages they are and the age I am, all the things we enjoy together, and I say, terrific, I like this. I'm so glad I had them when I did."

Judy looks back at the many books she wrote when her kids were small and doesn't exactly know how she managed it. She guesses it was because there weren't many diversions then. But she wouldn't trade her life now for anything. She may have been more prolific in the early days, but she didn't have nearly as much fun. "I love being forty," she says. "I look at beautiful young girls and admire them, but I know they don't really know much. I feel like I do."

Her children give her a great deal of personal satisfaction as well as pleasure. They are individuals with vivacious personalities whose company she enjoys. She admits to being less than perfect as a mother, saying, "My emotions often get in my way. But we do talk, freely and openly, about everything. On good days, I feel very proud of myself and think I must have done something right somewhere along the line. On bad days, I feel less guilty than I used to, realizing they are people responsible for their own actions. I hope I can continue to play an important part in their lives as they grow up and go away from home."

It's obvious that people are extremely important to Judy. "In my fantasy life, I am not a writer," she says. "I don't like sitting in that little room all by myself all day. I'd like to get dressed and go out to work and be a part of the mainstream. My editor friends say I'm crazy, that I'm living out their fantasy of being able to work at home. But they don't realize what they have. They are, after all, away from the HOUSE! A woman at home is considered a housewife no matter what else she is doing. A man writing at home is a WRITER and often has a wife to bring him coffee and see he is well cared for and not disturbed. Whose duty is it to see that I am well cared for? Oh, I would love a wife."

In spite of Judy's misgivings about the conflicts of career versus family and the solitary confinement necessary for writing, she admits there have been many satisfactions. "What delights me about a writing day," she says, "is humor. I can't set out to be funny, but when it happens spontaneously, it is so much fun! I'll just sit there and roar. It's not as if I'm patting myself on the back and saying, 'Oh, Judy, you're so clever.' It's 'Look what they're saying to each other.' The characters become so real to me that I refer to them at the dinner table as if they were good friends I'd been talking to that day."

Judy with Larry, Tom, and Randy (photo by Bill Gleasner)

Another satisfaction has been financial independence. It enabled her to escape an unhappy marriage and to support herself and her children. She's amazed that she turned out to be such a commercial success. "I write what I write and it happened to find a wide audience. It feels nice to be independent. I never, never want to go back to the other way."

While the constant flow of letters from her readers sustains her in her lonely work, recognition by juvenile literature experts also is important. The superb review that the

New York Times gave *Margaret* was her first great thrill; another came recently when she was asked to address the American Book Association Convention and ended up on the platform with two giants in the field of children's books: Maurice Sendak and Dr. Seuss.

In a wistful mood, she says, "There are times when I think I've done it all. I've done something special. I didn't know I was doing something special at the time, but looking back, I see that I have. Maybe that's it for me. Now it's time for other people to do what they can do."

Judy feels success can be very destructive if it comes too easily and too fast. "I would hate to have published my first book at an early age and have had it become a wild success," she says. "My success was very sweet. It developed slowly and was a personal success rather than something for the whole world to know about. It was very quiet. First the letters started to come from the children, then the recognition from the publishing world. It's not good to get thinking about success too much. Living outside the New York area is very healthy for me. I find I'm far less competitive with myself."

Blume books continue to sell, now totaling more than six million copies. Her agent is constantly being approached for movie and television rights, and the books have been translated into many languages. Even the English, who at first turned down her books as "unsuitable for British children," have purchased foreign rights.

Judy admits there are negatives to her success. "At the beginning, I told every neighbor about each sale. When it gets big, you can't do that. Who can share that with you? Your children, your spouse, your mother. When big money is involved, where aren't you going to find sour grapes? It becomes more sharing it with your agent and your editor. They can feel the joy with you. They care because they're involved in the project. It's kind of sad that while you're sharing yourself with more and more people through your books, you can personally share your happiness with fewer and fewer."

One big drawback to being a best-selling author is the feeling she gets from the public that they own her. "Their expectations are so out of line," she says, "and their requests so difficult to deal with. They say, 'Write this, don't write that. Don't ever write another book using this word.' They want me to produce the same book over and over. 'Don't disappoint us,' they say. Why don't they understand I am just like they are. I can't do any more than they can do. I feel they're just grabbing at me from all directions and that I need someone to protect me."

The very worst moment of her entire career was caused by a review. "My first review of *Iggie's House,* which is not a very good book, was so bad that had I not already written another book, I might have stopped writing altogether." But with succeeding books the reviews got better and better; some actually glowed. "Then came *Starring Sally J. Freedman as Herself,* a very important book to me. I thought it was my best effort, that I had done something that I hadn't done before."

"*Publisher's Weekly* ran a vicious review by a woman who'd been reviewing my books regularly and had been very fond of them. She said the book was sickening. I was devastated. That was when I grabbed my typewriter and lugged it to the edge of the canyon behind our home. I almost threw it in. You bare your soul to the world, and someone comes along and pours salt on your wounds. Who needs it? I remain every bit as vulnerable as I was in the beginning, maybe even more so."

Judy is often asked for advice about writing and getting published. She thinks people write out of their own needs rather than "deciding" to be a writer. She counsels beginners not to give up easily, to write what they really care about rather than just something to get published. "If it's very real to us as writers," she says, "it stands a better chance of being real to our readers." She feels there's nothing wrong with trying out all kinds of styles, but most important is to tell it in the most natural way. Self-discipline is paramount. "Keep going," she says. "You will grow. You will change. You will learn."

Her ideas, she says, come from everywhere. Her daughter Randy used to come home from school and tell her about some kids in her class who were tormenting a fat girl. That provided the inspiration for *Blubber*. Hearing some of the problems of a friend's daughter who had scoliosis inspired *Deenie*. She wrote *It's Not the End of the World* because so many families around her were suffering through divorces. The character, Fudge, in *Tales of a Fourth Grade Nothing* was based on her son Larry, but it wasn't Larry who swallowed the pet turtle. That she read about in the newspaper.

Once she has the idea for the story, Judy carries it in her head for a long time before sitting down at the typewriter. She knows something about the basic situation, her main character, and where she thinks she's going (although often it changes as the story develops). "I think best with paper and pencil," she says, "making many, many notes to myself. When I finally sit down to type, I work very haphazardly."

Her first drafts are very rough, and her characters develop gradually. Often they don't become "real" people until she starts to rewrite. She describes doing a first draft as "torture" and admits that if she thinks in terms of a whole book at the beginning, she might panic.

But she says she likes to rewrite and rarely has to redo the dialogue. "I can make people talk to each other, and it usually comes out right the first time." She learned how to approach second, third, and fourth drafts from Dick

Jackson, her editor at Bradbury Press. His method was to ask her many, many questions because he contended she knew more about her characters than showed in her writing. In fact, when she was writing *Wifey*, she didn't have that kind of input, so she pretended Dick was in the room shooting question after question at her.

Judy's been lucky to have some editorial help right at home. Her daughter Randy has, according to Judy, "a terrific editorial sense." As an expert on what kids say to each other, she's helped her mother change some dialogue that didn't sound natural to her age group. Randy has been in on every manuscript her mother has produced from the first draft right on to the final one.

In spite of the pain of the first draft, Judy tends to forget the difficulties easily. "Writing books," she says, "is like having a baby because once it's done you only remember what a joy it was. You catch yourself saying, 'Oh, I had such a good time writing that book.' Then I have to pinch myself and say, 'Wait a minute. That's not true.' I have read about people who say, 'Just give me a typewriter and put me in that room and I'm so happy.' I don't feel that way at all. It's hard, hard work. Yes, some things flow out beautifully, but most don't. For me writing gets more difficult with each book. I want to be as good as I was before, and things aren't all fresh and new now."

Judy feels it's very important to grow, to try new challenges and not to give in to the public's demand to write the same book over and over. Mostly, she wants to go on producing work that touches people's lives.

When she wrote *Wifey*, she took a giant step. Highly regarded as an author of children's books, she plunged into the uncharted depths of adult novels. She's glad she did. "I'm very proud of *Wifey*," she says. "It was difficult, but it's something I very much wanted to do."

When she started writing *Wifey,* she spent lots of time second-guessing herself. Was she writing an adult story in juvenile form? Was the tone right? Were the characters convincing? The first forty pages took three months to write, so it was with great satisfaction that she finally held the finished hardcover book in her hands. She'd done what she set out to do, what many people had advised her against. An added bonus was that now adults have begun to write and say, "I feel so much better, knowing someone else knows how I feel."

The book received quite a bit of advance publicity, most of it alluding to the explicit sex scenes. Judy's mother worried, "Will I be able to face my friends? Will I be able to hold up my head on North Broad Street?" After Mrs. Sussman read the book, she said, "I understand you better now." Judy kept saying, "Mother, it's not me. It's fiction." Her mother replied, "O.K., you can say that, but there are things in there that I recognize as you. And I wish I had been able to help you in your suffering at the time."

Wifey deals with very familiar territory for Judy; it describes a suburban New Jersey housewife trapped in an unhappy marriage. "I think," Judy says, "I've written about the kind of person I was and could have remained if I had not met up with the good fortune of finding this career."

Fortunately for many loyal readers of all ages, Judy did discover her talent, pursue her craft, and ride out the rough places that might have silenced a weaker person. She confesses that she's always looking for a way out of her career, except when she takes down a book that she has written.

Then she thinks, "Oh, how wonderful. I wrote this. How did I ever do it?"

Erma Bombeck

W<small>HO IS</small> E<small>RMA</small> B<small>OMBECK</small>?

In her own words: "I am basically a woman who has gone through life with my pantyhose on backwards. I'm the wife of the husband no one wants to swap with."

Erma Bombeck is a writer whose column is syndicated in more than seven hundred papers, an author whose books ride the crest of the best-selling lists. She is a sought-after speaker who commands many thousands of dollars for a performance. A TV regular on "Good Morning, America" and "The Tonight Show," she also creates, writes, and produces her own television specials.

Can this dynamic career woman really describe herself as a dowdy housewife who spends most of her time in the fetal position nipping on the vanilla? Yes, of course she can. Erma Bombeck can do, and has done, just about anything. But the thing she does best is to make people laugh.

Is Erma's life funnier than anyone else's? Childhood memories of winos slumping in the doorways of her neighborhood in Dayton, Ohio, suggest that it isn't. But the

43

way she views the trials of daily existence is. "I was too stupid to know we were poor," she says. "I'd just have worried myself sick if I'd known. But I thought it was a really neat neighborhood." Her best friend lived over the funeral parlor, and for entertainment they attended the synagogue on Saturdays and the Catholic church on Sundays. Erma was Protestant at the time.

Her mother, also named Erma, gave birth to Erma at the age of sixteen. Her father, Cassius Fiste, was a laborer who died when she was nine years old. Erma describes her mother as "a survivor, one of the gutsiest ladies around." A young widow at twenty-five whose education ended with fourth grade, she worked on the General Motors assembly line to support herself and her child. Asked if she, too, has a sense of humor, Erma's mother nods her head toward her famous daughter and replies, "I had her, didn't I?"

Even though their financial situation was grim, her mother insisted Erma take dancing lessons. "My mother wanted me to sing and dance my way out of poverty like Shirley Temple. It didn't matter that I had no talent and my hips were saddlebags," says Erma. Still fairly unfazed by her daughter's writing accomplishments, her mom is proudest when she's on TV. When she watched Erma waltz around the stage in the arms of John Denver on a posh TV special, she said, "Well, Erma finally made it in show business."

She never did understand her daughter's interest in reading. When other girls were trading Nancy Drew mysteries, Erma was checking books out of the library by such noted humorists as James Thurber, H. Allen Smith, and Robert Benchley. She wrote poetry and harbored dreams of becoming a writer. "My mom doesn't like to read," says Erma. "She doesn't understand books at all, and yet, God bless her, she shot the whole Christmas budget one year by buying a book I wanted that cost five dollars."

When Erma was fourteen, the correspondent Dorothy Thompson came to Dayton to lecture. Erma spent her last nickel to hear her speak even though she had a fever. She infected the entire hall with measles that night but remembers she "was absolutely ruthless" in her need to see Ms. Thompson.

Newspapers fascinated her. At the vocational high school where she alternated two weeks of classes with two weeks of work, she contributed humor to the school paper. Her part-time job as a copy girl at the *Dayton Journal-Herald* gave Erma a taste for the world of journalism, and she eventually was able to convince the editor to let her write. After high school, she worked a year full time at the *Herald* while she accumulated enough money to enter college. She was able to pay her way through school by arranging her classes at the University of Dayton so she was free to work in the afternoon. Not only was Erma the first high school graduate in her family, she was the only one of twenty-eight cousins who made it all the way through college.

A conscientious student who took her studies seriously, Erma learned a great deal about writing during her school years. "Writing is communication," she says, "and there is no better way of saying something than being right up front and expressing yourself in uncluttered sentences."

She'll never forget the journalism teacher who taught her that. "I had written a very wordy essay," she remembers, "and his response was to ask me to bring him a Bible. When I brought it to him, he asked me to open it to the first page and read. I read, 'In the beginning God created the heaven and the earth.' Then he stopped me and asked if I understood it. I said yes. 'Every word?' he asked. 'Did you understand every word?' I nodded yes.

'That's the way to write,' he said, 'being absolutely straightforward and saying exactly what you mean without trying to impress anyone.'"

Erma admits every once in a while her English degree gets in the way and she goes for the big words. "Oh, I have words," she chuckles. "Some even have three syllables." But then she remembers that open Bible and says to herself, "Hold it, Erma; stick with basic conversational English."

After receiving her college diploma, she joined the *Herald* on a full-time basis. Fellow workers remember her "as the bouncy copy girl in bobby socks, pleated skirts, and baggy sweaters who found humor in everything." Gradually, she worked her way up from compiling radio listings and writing obituaries to being a reporter for the women's page. She even wrote a satirical column on housework titled "Operation Dustrag," but she doesn't think it was really appreciated. "In the forties," she says, "housework was considered a religious experience."

In 1949, Erma married Bill Bombeck, whom she'd first met in high school and who also had worked part-time as a copy editor. Her job at the *Herald* kept them in groceries while Bill went to college, making up for the time he'd lost serving in the army. When he began his teaching career, Erma stayed home to start a family. The years that followed were full of the frustration and tribulations that go with raising children and keeping house. "For eleven years," she says, "I lived in the suburbs, putting on weight, overbleaching my clothes, and watching my yellow wax build up." It was not that she had an identity problem. After all, she was well known in car-pool circles as the "Tuesday pickup with the hole in the muffler."

Her memories aren't all that lighthearted. The Bombecks bought an acre of land and planned to put a house on it. "A small house was all we could afford," Erma recalls. "We later learned the neighbors had circulated a petition to keep us from building because our house wasn't considered 'appropriate' for the area. They thought our little two-bedroom frame would detract from the larger, more impressive brick homes around us. The people never did become friendly, and, mercifully, we only stayed there a short time. Years later, I gave a speech, and one of the women who lived in that neighborhood came up to meet me afterwards. 'If I'd known you were going to be so damn funny,' she said, 'I would have spoken to you when we were neighbors.' "

Erma kept her sanity by exercising her sense of humor and later, in a friendly neighborhood, by enjoying a back-and-forth-between-houses camaraderie with other young mothers. They had a great deal in common. Most, like Erma, were involved in daily skirmishes that resulted from being "overworked, overchildrened, and underpatienced."

Not a minute of that time was wasted. Later, she would realize that period of her life was first-hand research, a mother lode of motherhood she would later mine for pay. "The fact is," she says, "that most of the stuff that I find funniest is not what's happening now but the things that happened back then, you know, in retrospect. Any pain has vanished, and now I've got pure humor to draw from."

Her husband was her lifeline to "the real world." Bill Bombeck was a young assistant high school principal whose career was moving rapidly ahead. Erma remembers those years nostalgically: "I had such pride in my husband's career. I lived through him and didn't think there was anything wrong with that. It was the thing to do, the way we lived — vicariously. We'd sit around and talk about our husbands all the time. If he was a very good husband, he'd occasionally say, 'That was a good meal,' 'the kids look nice today,' or 'here, let me do that; you look tired.' Even if he didn't say it, it didn't upset me because that was my job."

Three children under five can try the strongest sense of humor, but Erma's memories of those years are predominantly positive. For one thing, she says, "I never felt like a second-class citizen even when I was doing the crud detail. It wasn't part of my life. I never felt put down or was made to feel dumb, which I think a lot of women are. When you're raising children, you're in such an isolated world. You go to the grocery story every week, run the car pools, and devote your life to your kids. It's so intense; that's all you do. But as negatively as I write about kids sometimes, as much of a chore as it was to raise them and keep house, I really enjoyed that time."

Erma's unique way of looking at life's frustrations made the difference. She remembers going into the kitchen one morning and finding one kid going through the clothes hamper looking for something to wear while another announced he was a participle in the school play and needed a costume. The bank called to tell her the check she'd written to the paper boy had bounced, she tried to catch the dog to wipe the catsup off his paws, and her husband refused to take his lunch in a box with the seven dwarfs on it. "I turned to my daughter," wrote Erma, "and said, 'Someday, dear, all this will be yours.' "

Erma remembers how she and her friends maintained their sanity. They covered rolls of toilet tissue with yarn, made Christmas wreaths out of macaroni, and took every course in the YWCA catalogue from exercise to cake decorating. "We kept busy, busy, busy," she says, "filling up the time and being exhausted."

Still it wasn't enough, and Erma knew she had to do something else. In 1963, when the youngest of her three children entered kindergarten, she thought about going back to work. She says she shared the same insecurities other women with growing children face. She had reached the point where she thought she couldn't do anything but get stains out of bibs. Ads that announced the opportunity to "Earn money — address envelopes at one cent apiece" made her wonder, "Could I do that? Could I?"

The decision to do "something else," according to Erma, was an easy one. "At thirty-seven," she says, "I got up off my knees and said to the dog, 'I do not feel fulfilled changing toilet tissue spindles.' " She decided to write a humor column because she was "too old for a paper route, too young for social security, and too tired for an affair."

She showed a few sample columns to the editor of their suburban weekly paper, the *Kettering Oakwood Times*. Selecting what she would write about was simple because she said, "Being a housewife was the only thing in life I could discuss for more than ten minutes." The editor agreed to run the column and pay her three dollars a week, an arrangement that lasted three years. "I was so happy with three dollars a week," she remembers, "just to see my name. It was an ego trip in a sense."

It also lifted her out of stifling household drudgery. Erma understands full well what keeps other women from trying to break out of the housewife syndrome even after their kids are grown. "It's because they have dreams," she explains. "They have to have dreams, or they wouldn't survive. The secret is that in the back of their minds they're saying, 'I'll write a book someday, once I get the dishes done, the shelf paper changed, and the kitchen painted.' They keep putting it off for a reason. If they do it, and they fail, they have nothing left to dream about. When the time comes that you have to do it, you put it all on the line. You are taking the chance of not having any dreams left."

Erma in the laundry room (photo by Paul Degruccio)

Luckily, Erma's dream carried her beyond her wildest expectations. The man responsible for propelling Erma's career from a local success to a national one was the editor of the *Dayton Journal-Herald.* "I owe everything to Glenn Thompson," she says. He read one of her columns in the suburban weekly and asked her to do two columns a week for his editorial page. Glenn was so impressed with her work he sent it, unbeknownst to Erma, on to the Newsday Syndicate with a note saying he thought she deserved a wider audience. "This little column was a success," she says with wonder, "from day one. It was in the *Journal-Herald* three weeks when they sold it to a syndicate, which has to be a record. It got thirty-eight papers the first year. I can only think of two or three papers we lost, and they ended up buying it back. It was just phenomenal. I was extremely lucky to be in the right place at the right time."

Glenn Thompson would not take anything for his part in her success. She says, "He just sat back and watched it all happen and said that was enough for him. I can't believe anybody other than my mother would have done this much for me."

"The column," she says affectionately, "is my fat cat. It will always be my first priority. I have not gotten bored with it all. I still love doing it." She gives it credit for the rest of her career. Because of the column, she was invited to speak to groups, write books of humor, go on book tours, and appear on talk shows. Her success on these shows led to her regular appearances on ABC TV's "Good Morning, America" and "The Tonight Show." The latest opportunity has been a chance to produce her own TV specials. All this from four hundred and fifty words three times a week!

Those who read her short column sometimes guess that it comes right off the top of her head. Erma recognizes that reaction as an extremely naive opinion from someone who has never written professionally. "The column goes through several drafts," she says. "There is considerable polishing and honing before I let go of it. I don't work for one out of three columns. I work for three out of three. I don't always get it, but I'm working for it. If you are really serious about writing, you have to give it the number-one priority in your life. A lot of people are not willing to do that. It owns you. It's something that comes before the dishes are done, the beds are made; it comes when you're in the hospital, when you come home from funerals. It comes at inopportune moments of your life."

"I have not talked to any writer who says, 'It flows.' Nothing flows. It's such hard work. I don't know if people really realize that. I've worked on things for two full days, and finally I say to myself, 'O.K., this doesn't work. Get rid of it.' I hate that. I get hysterical, cry a little, and throw it away. I look at the wastebasket, and I think, *There are two days of my life.* But if it doesn't work, it doesn't work. The moment you start compromising with a column, you're in trouble. Everything has to be the best you can do."

Erma has been doing the best she can three times a week for fifteen years. She's impatient with novelists who talk of making their own hours and waiting for inspiration. "Most of them," she says, "don't do dishes, make beds, go to the store every three hours, or sort socks. I don't have their kind of luxury. I hit the post office on Friday with three columns whether I feel like it or not. To say, 'Well, I write when I really get into it' is a bunch of bull. Put the paper in the typewriter, stare at it a long time, get snowblindness if you have to, but write something."

She says that people get hung up on style. "A lot of writers ask me how you develop style. You don't. It develops you. It's your own personal way of saying something. When someone reads something that has no name on it, they know you wrote it because you have a unique way of writing. Beginning writers worry about all the wrong things. They should worry about communicating."

Erma is completely disciplined. She has to be. "I can't tell eight hundred editors, 'Hey, fellas, I'm having a bad day. I've got a headache, and my dog died.' They won't buy that. I get letters from women saying they'd like to write a column because they have four hours of free time now that the kids are in school, and they really could use the money. Oh, boy, they don't realize it's a full-time job that requires total discipline."

Asked what quality is most essential for a professional writer, Erma shoots back, "Good health," without hesitation. It takes a great deal of stamina to write, but even when she is sick, she turns out copy. She's written in a hospital bed while in pain from a kidney infection. "When I hurt," she says matter-of-factly, "I don't cry. I write four hundred and fifty words."

Erma has her own theories as to the source of her drive. She thinks it's born in her basic insecurity. She says, "It shows in every word I write." She is afraid someone might think that what she does isn't such a big deal and challenge her position as America's favorite female humor writer. "Every single column I write must be the very best I can possibly do," she explains, "or else someone is going to slip right up here and take my place."

Keeping her number-one position is what propels Erma to her desk at 7:30 sharp and keeps her there until 2 P.M. She knows when it's two, she says, because that's when her head splits open. Sometimes she wonders if she can pull it off again. Then she realizes that kind of worrying is not productive and that, above all else, she must produce. So she pulls herself together and gives the column her best shot.

As a seasoned columnist, she now has fewer self-doubts, but she remembers the early years well. When she first started writing, she would ask Bill to comment on everything she wrote. After she would read a column to him, he would sometimes question the wisdom of a particular reference. Erma would be stricken. "I would defend every single word. I really didn't want criticism at all; I wanted him to say it was terrific. But he was too honest."

Rejection is a fact of a writer's life. She says, "If you don't know how to live with it, you don't know what it's all about. Just having someone say, 'I don't like what you've done; it isn't funny,' hurts. You put up with a whole lot of that. I've had enough to know how much it hurts and how it reduces you."

Erma's secret is that she doesn't stay reduced. She's bothered less by critics now than previously. She realizes they are a part of life that isn't going to go away. When launching into something new, she knows she's exposing herself to criticism. Yet she's learned that she needs new

Erma relaxing (photo by Bill Gleasner)

challenges to grow and use her talents to the fullest.

If someone had told her she would one day be on national TV on a regular basis, she would have said, "I can't
do that. I'm too shy." In fact, the first time Erma was to
appear on "The Tonight Show," she paced up and down
the hotel room telling her mother she couldn't go through
with it. She was scared and felt like spitting up. Her
mother told her she probably couldn't do it if she were going to go out there pretending to be something she wasn't.
But she added, "If you just go out there, be honest, and
do the best you can, I know you can do it."

Erma says she was "really lousy" on that first show. "I
didn't freeze," she says, "but I didn't have any funny
lines. I just sat there in a stupor and was saved by Johnny
and one of the other guests." But she did survive it, and
now she does beautifully on television. When she is
behind what she describes as those "god-awful curtains in
Burbank" waiting to face the lights and millions of view-
ers, she remembers her mother's advice. She is calm
because she is prepared, and she is herself, the relaxed
professional self that has evolved out of years of experience before the cameras.

Erma has developed a way of coping with criticism. She
can't afford to let every little snide remark disturb her, or
she couldn't function, so her mail is divided into two cate-
gories, signed and unsigned.

"If you don't sign your name, you don't get read," she
says. "I sign my name. I stand here in my underwear and
take responsibility for what I write, and unless you do,
too, I won't read it." Legitimate criticism that keeps her
in touch with her readers is another thing. "If you do sign
your name," she says, "it depends on what we're talking
about. If I have truly offended you on something that you
feel very strongly about then I am truly sorry. I really am.
I don't care how funny I thought the column was; if I

The Bombeck family: Bill, Erma, Matt, Betsy, and Andy

bothered someone to the point where they're really upset, I'll write a letter and apologize. I won't apologize for the column but I am sorry you found it offensive. Sometimes I back down totally and say, 'You're right. I should not have written this. It's a sensitive area, and I had no business being there.' I make a lot of mistakes, so I listen if it's legitimate and if it's going to help me in the future as to what I'm going to write. It's not always an easy thing to find that middle of the road."

Erma's readership covers a huge segment of the populace, which she says runs "from teenagers to two days before death." Ninety percent of the job is finding a topic that might appeal to all of them at one time. She has opinions on numerous topics that are not for the column. Many subjects, she feels, just cannot be handled humorously. In general, she sticks close to home, regaling readers with quips on family life. "My beat," she once wrote, "is the utility room."

She knows that if she listens to those who urge her to use her column to put across a message, she'll lose her audience. "I don't have a message," she says. "I write to make myself feel better. I started the column out of sheer boredom, and one reason it is read is that people want relief from the grimness they find in the rest of the paper. They want to laugh at something."

The utility-room beat is not without its many areas of sensitivity. A column she did on the fun large families have drew fire from ecology-minded readers for weeks. When she poked fun at the custom of wearing name tags at conventions, she said she found it hard to socialize with people "who spend thirty minutes or so talking to my left bosom." Some papers changed "bosom" to shoulder. It bothered her. "I meant bosom," she says adamantly. Once an editor told her not to use the word "bathroom" again or she'd drop the column. She defended her use of the word. "Being a mother," she says, "is like being a doctor. Words like 'bathroom'—you just rip 'em off."

Erma gets plenty of positive reactions to her work to counter the effects of the censors and the critics. She has legions of fans who love her and write warm letters to tell her so. "They regard me with a familiarity that is really flattering," she says. Most of them feel she knows so much about their lives that she must be nearby. In Ireland, readers go into the *Dublin News* and ask to speak with her. They think she must be an Irish housewife.

The housewife from Ohio who set out to ward off boredom and perhaps give people a laugh or two in the process has accomplished far more. She says, "I've had letters from people who have gone through deep depression or cancer operations, people who have lost their husbands and decided they wanted to join the living again because they read one of my books. That's got to be the most flattering thing in the world. One woman, hoping to bring

her husband and son back together, handed them one of
my serious columns about relationships. It helped them
gain a new understanding of the other's position, and
they reconciled their differences. A few months later, the
father died. The mother wrote thanking me for helping
bring peace to the family during those last precious
months."

Her books' popularity speaks eloquently of their wide
appeal. *At Wit's End, Just Wait Till You Have Children
of Your Own!, I Lost Everything in the Post-Natal Depression, The Grass is Always Greener Over the Septic
Tank, If Life is Just a Bowl of Cherries, What Am I Doing
in the Pits,* and *Aunt Erma's Cope Book* have all been excellent sellers.

Many critics have responded enthusiastically to Erma
Bombeck's unique contribution. A typical assessment
that appeared in *Best Sellers* said, "There are those who
write about...suburban things with cynicism, snarling
and spleen. Erma doesn't. She manages with the deftness
of a trapeze artist to come up with a smile on her face in
the midst of unaccountable maneuvers. She takes joy and
strength from the things she satirizes. We need more of
that."

"All I do is watch the human condition," Erma says,
"and write it down. It's like stealing. Why wouldn't anyone want to write humor? It's happy work. It makes people happy; it makes you happy. You just pick it off the
wall." She says the only part that requires talent is observation. "It's a perception that some people just seem to
have. You watch people, you see the frustrations, take a
slice, and go with it. I think observation is most of it."

She can't explain just where the ideas come from or
how they develop. "I just have a feeling for something
that is going to amuse people and through the process of
trying things out, I realize that the only person I can make

Erma writing a check (photo by Paul Degruccio)

fun of is myself." She loves to play around with dialogue or take a little topic and run with it.

The human condition she's observed most closely has been in her own home. In the early years, the column centered almost exclusively around the exploits of her family. How does she get away with this typical Bombeckian anecdote? When she asked one toddler to put a loaf of bread in her grocery cart, he said he didn't know which one was theirs. "You can't miss it," she told him. "It has your baby brother in it." Sure enough, he put it in the wrong cart. She thought to herself, *I have a swift one on my hands.*

Erma admits she lifts situations from her husband and children's lives but says they never objected. She's been careful never to give her kids' names or ages in the column or to reveal private things about their lives. "They all have a wonderful sense of humor, and they're the first to realize what the readers don't—that the columns are semifictional."

Erma insists humor is a very personal, extremely subjective thing. When she writes a column, she relies on her readers to "take as much out of it as you want to. The kids aren't mine. They're yours. The husband isn't mine. He's yours. You've got to do it yourself. I can lay all kinds of lines on you. If you don't relate, and you're in a bad mood, or if it touches too close to home, you're not going to laugh. You have to provide the humor."

The real-life Bombeck family is refreshingly typical. Erma used to carry a lot of guilt when she left home to give a speech or promote a book. "My kids gave me a bad time," she says, "because I was such a pushover for it. I could stay home for months, and nothing would happen. But the minute I left, there was a crisis. Once when I was out of town, my daughter wrecked the car and had her license suspended. To her chagrin, it was announced the next day in the local paper's headlines. Why? Because her name was Bombeck. I decided it was a good lesson. 'O.K., kids, you better shape up,' we told them, 'or you're going to read about it in the paper.' "

When reporters ask Matt, Andy, and Betsy what it's like having a famous mother, they never know just how to answer because they've never had any other kind. "They meet well-known people," Erma says, "and they're impressed, but they can't imagine what anyone famous would be doing at our house. The fact that it amazes them is refreshing."

Erma's the first to admit the kids have not been perfect, but she and Bill have a fine relationship with them. Now that they're out of the nest, she finds she's enjoying them in a whole new way. She says, "When you see this child become a fine human being that you've had a share in molding, it's great. All of a sudden, there's something coming back."

One of Erma's trips had a great impact on the Bombecks. In 1971, she flew to Arizona to give a speech. Having left Chicago in the midst of a blizzard, she was pleasantly surprised to deplane into a warm breeze in Phoenix. She went home aglow with enthusiasm for the Southwest. But the family was settled on the farm in Ohio they had always wanted, or thought they wanted. Now Bill and Erma were discovering it was not what they wanted, after all. Complete with a large house and horses for the kids, it was taking all their energy just trying to keep up with everything. After much discussion, the couple decided it was a good time to relocate the family, that they were ready for a warmer climate and a different life style.

Before the move, there was some hesitation on the part of the children. But soon after their arrival, they became great fans of the area. And why not? Life in Paradise Valley, Arizona, was not too hard to take. Their lovely home had a swimming pool and tennis court as well as a spectacular view of the mountains.

By this time, Erma was reaping great financial rewards for her efforts. Her educator husband is underpaid, she says, while she is overpaid. She admits to being embarrassed when she realizes they can afford so much now but can't break the habit of looking at price tags. The Bombecks have agreed not to deny their children "the poverty they so richly deserve." Each has had to buy and maintain his or her own car, yet she asks, "How do you tell your kid to get up a 4 A.M. and work his paper route when you know you can afford to let him sleep?"

Although Erma can now afford a secretary and a woman to help with the cleaning, she is fiercely possessive of her domesticity. How did she celebrate a paperback rights sale for a million dollars? She says, "I didn't do the laundry for three days. I've got to scrub the john, and I've got to make the beds. And it isn't just that I don't want the column to be a sham. I believe in all this stuff — raising kids and being a good housewife."

Erma doesn't expect her family to keep up with her career. "They don't read anything," she says. "It doesn't bother me. I don't need that kind of stuff from the family. They're not there to feed your ego every three hours. It's not their job."

But they never know when they're apt to run into their ubiquitous mother's work. "Last year," recalls Erma, "when my son was teaching fourth grade, he needed something to keep the kids quiet just before the holidays. He happened to pick up *Reader's Digest* and read 'On the Twelve Days of School.' When he reached the end, he was amazed to see my name. 'Good grief,' he said. 'My mother wrote this!' They said, 'Yeah, yeah, Mr. Bombeck,' thinking he was kidding. But he was genuinely surprised."

Erma is especially sensitive to Bill's position as husband of a well-known woman. "I guess I cool it on purpose," she says. "He never sees any of my clippings. I think it can get out of hand when one career is more flashy than the other. If I get an award or an honorary doctorate, I mention it to him. But I guess I don't play it up a lot. I think it could get to be a real pain. Sometimes I ask for his advice on financial matters, and when I'm on "The Tonight Show," he stays up to watch it. But he never goes with me when I lecture or do a book tour."

"What we have done is protect each other. When he was chaperoning school activities, he'd say, 'You don't have to go to that football game or sit through another performance of Gilbert and Sullivan.' So I started doing the same thing. There's nothing more boring than having to sit through a speech you've heard fifty times before. I wouldn't put him through that. So we sort of separate when I'm being professional and doing my thing. We get together for our personal lives. It's awfully hard to have a

Erma speaking at Rosary College (photo by Kevin Horan)

personal life where you keep a lot of things out of it, but I think we've done a pretty good job."

Some problems are unavoidable."You can't imagine how insensitive some people can be to the spouse who's not in the limelight. I have attended gatherings with Bill, and people have totally ignored this extremely bright and very funny man. I think it's terrible, and I hate it. The ideal situation is to be with friends who appreciate us both. Some people are good about it. They don't expect me to be funny all the time, and they don't care if I'm writing a book. They just say, 'Shut up, Erma.' Wistfully, she adds, "You know, if you get a couple of good friends in this life, it's a lot."

Erma's schedule doesn't leave much time to cultivate friendships. Sometimes she feels one-dimensional, that all she does is work. Her deadlines have cornered her into be-

An autographing session

ing a loner a good share of the time, and she'd like more leisure for socializing. Especially missed is the stimulation of other women that she enjoyed when her children were small. But Erma admits she's been saying the same thing for more than ten years. "Every time I make myself some time," she admits with a sigh, "I fill it up with other commitments."

Work consumes every day of the week. For a while, she tried to play tennis but could only play at "weird" times, when the writing was going well and all her deadlines had been met. She decided she just couldn't ask other people to work around her schedule all the time, so she gave it up. "It's not that I'm unathletic," she hastens to add. "I can extract the racket from the press very well."

She manages her writing time by doing the columns during the week and the books on weekends. Her idea of pleasure does not quite fit the woman who has written that she never learned to cook because she thought it was a fad. "If the work has gone well during the week," she says, "and Sunday has been productive (which means the chapter I've been working on comes off well), then I knock off early. I cook up a lovely dinner for just the two of us. It's a nice feeling. That's my relaxation."

One of the reasons Erma has not become bored by this steady diet of work is that so many things keep changing. "Imagine being locked in the utility room forever!" she says, her eyes rolling. Luckily, Erma experienced a change in her life that coincided with the general change in the status of women.

"My kids always thought of me as a mother, housewife, and cook," she says. "I was doing all this other stuff, and it didn't matter to them. A lot of mothers were away from home playing bridge, but I would be away giving a speech in Cleveland. They didn't really care what I was doing as long as I made the Girl Scout meeting and got dinner on the table. People are so naive when they say young kids are proud of you. Kids are so self-centered that they only think, *How does this affect me.*"

"I think Andy was maybe fourteen or fifteen when he came into the kitchen to ask me to make him a sandwich. I told him the kitchen was closed and to make his own if he wanted one. He looked at me and said, 'Hey, that's your job.' I had been syndicated for many, many years and had written a couple of books and was feeling pretty secure in my own right. I thought about it a minute. Then I sat him down and told him what my job was and that it wasn't running around after him."

Gradually, her kids grew up and left home. Erma also began to emerge and discovered, "There was a whole big world out there to write about. It worked very well," she says. "Because if I'd tried to remain just a domestic columnist, I'd be in a lot of trouble. But women still have children, and they still have houses, although their attitudes towards both have changed. It's been a blessing for me. Everything affects you, and you have to change. I don't know any columnists who read the same year after year. If they do, they're in trouble."

One of the most profound changes in Erma has been her attitude toward the women's movement. She admits to being threatened initially by the revolutionaries who spearheaded the liberation. "I was scared to death," she said. "Their thinking was so foreign to me. I didn't make up the stereotypes. I'm fifty-one, and I was born to them. I was stubborn and maybe a little pompous at first. I had a narrow viewpoint. When I shut up and started listening, I realized a lot of good has come out of the movement.

"Some things are still uncomfortable. I know homosexuals and lesbians exist, but I don't know how to explain the situation, and I don't always know how to handle it. But I do know they're people, and ignoring them is not going to make them go away. We all live in this country and pay taxes. They have rights just as black people and handicapped people have rights. You get a little more comfortable with some of these ideas as you live with them. Soon you're not threatened by them anymore."

Always the champion of the beleaguered housewife, Erma resented the women's movement in its early stages for ignoring the domestic community. "Everyone became an authority on what the housewife wanted and needed," she said. "Everyone, that is, except the housewife. They picked us out as a battleground for the whole movement, but they didn't invite us to the war. We were the last to be asked what we wanted." During the question period after her speeches, women would ask her if she'd burned her bra yet. Erma answered, "I took a halfway measure; I scorched mine on the ironing board."

Suddenly, the housewife found herself in the eye of the liberation hurricane. Nothing she did was right. "If she complained," wrote Erma, "she was neurotic; if she didn't, she was stupid. If she stayed home with her children, she was boring and smothering; if she went out to work, she was selfish. When she discussed her future, her husband became depressed; when she discussed her past, she became depressed."

Many women were not ready for change. Erma pointed out that they were afraid of the price they would pay for exploring the territory outside the home. Some felt that though they might gain a career, they would lose a husband, that the penalty for fulfillment during the day would be exhaustion and resentment at night. "Will they feel too inadequate to run General Motors," she wrote, "but too educated to ever again sort socks?"

Ready or not, housewives everywhere were affected by changing attitudes. Although some used the women's movement as a long-awaited ticket out of the kitchen, others were painfully confused. Erma's prose took a serious turn when she spoke for women pulled in so many directions: "We apologized to our children for going back to school. Or worse, we filled our lives with busy work instead of doing what we were capable of doing. We resigned ourselves to the fact that anyone can raise children and keep house instead of asserting some are good at it and some women are lousy. We never organized, so that no one really knew what we felt, what we wanted, or what we really are."

Erma knew. She had done the whole bit — the toddlers, the toilets, and the Tupperware parties. Housewives wrote her tons of letters in which they articulated their thoughts, their dreams, and their frustrations because they knew she understood them. If ever there was a spokeswoman for the housewife, it was the columnist whose rallying cry was "Hey, let's look at us. We're all in

Erma relaxing in hotel room (photo by Bill Gleasner)

this mess together. Let's get some fun out of it."

Erma was a natural for the Women's Advisory Committee, a group of female leaders who advise the president on women. With characteristic modesty, she says, "My position on the committee is very Minnie Mouse, but I believe strongly in what we're trying to do." When asked to identify herself in a working session with the president, she simply said she was "Erma, a nonviolent mother."

Why did this busy woman who hated lonely hotel rooms on the lecture circuit agree to stump for the Equal Rights Amendment? Certainly it wasn't for money since there's none involved. "I'm an optimist," she explains. "I feel if I reach one person, it's all worthwhile. If just one woman says, 'You know, I think she makes some sense. She seems to care about her family and to have some decent values left. Maybe there's some truth in what she's saying.' I don't necessarily want her to get out and work for ERA. I just want her to go to the polls and cast a vote for herself. If one woman realizes the worth she has who never realized it before, if she'll take a chance on herself, then it's worth it. That's what it's all about."

In laundromats, in civic auditoriums, Erma speaks to small groups and large, telling her audiences about the Equal Rights Amendment. She describes the amendment as the twenty-four most misunderstood words since "one size fits all." Quick to assure her listeners that she, too, was once part of the great silent majority who sat back "and watched the libbers do battle," she says her changed attitude toward the women's movement put her in a very good position to tell them what's going on. Erma tries not to scare off women whose lives are comfortable and who are afraid of change. But she explains that if they want equal pay, think homemakers should get a fair shake, and don't believe in child abuse or wife beating, they must be named in the constitution in order to implement a program.

A woman all too familiar with unisex bathrooms on one flight after another, Mrs. Bombeck's great reward after touring for ERA is to finally head for home. Unfortunately, home is not always the peaceful haven she'd like. Sometimes strangers stop after seeing her house from a sightseeing bus and knock on her door hoping to see this famous humorist in person. She does everything she can to protect herself and her family from this kind of intrusion. When asked to open her house for a home tour once, she refused even though it was for a charitable cause. "I share about everything else," she says, "but that little gate out front, that's all the privacy I have left."

The real Erma Bombeck lives there. It's the nest from which she launches herself into a world that badly needs the laughs she has to give. What gives her home meaning is her husband. She tells her audiences that she doesn't know why their marriage has lasted so long, but she suspects it's because they've never had a meaningful conversation in their entire lives. In a more serious mood, she describes him as secure and unique, a man who adjusts to things gracefully. "I don't have to be funny around him. We can let go. Every once in a while we scream and shout, and that's great. Bill is everything in my life, the whole show."

Does he share her sense of humor? His idea of humor, she says, is to tell her he's been to the library and that all her books are in. He dedicated his doctoral thesis "To my wife Erma whose cold coffee and lousy lunches have forced me to return to employment." Erma says, "All the Bombecks have good senses of humor, but Bill's is the very best. Dry and droll. I love it. I feel that if a couple can still laugh after thirty years, they've either got something going or they're demented. Please don't ask me to decide which."

When asked the secret of her success, Erma shrugs and says, "I don't take myself too seriously. I don't take too many things seriously. I'm uncomplicated. I just sort of plod along, and if I run into a major setback, it's just like being poor. I'm too stupid to know it. When someone rejects what I do, I say O.K. and try it again. Before I tackle something new, I listen to a lot of people and ask endless questions. Then I go out and give it my best shot."

In the process, Erma has done a lot of growing. "I have found things about myself, things I can do that I never dreamed I would do, and that's the fun part of it," she says. "I still don't have a lot of confidence in myself, but I have a lot more than I used to. Everyone wants to have one thing that they feel they can do really well. I wasn't the brightest, the fastest, or the most beautiful. I guess what my career has given me is what I want for everyone else—a good feeling about myself."

Erma may describe herself as an overweight woman with crooked teeth who is somewhere between estrogen and death. But to her fans she is a well-loved symbol of courage and fortitude. If Erma can cope with the vicissitudes of life and come up chuckling, then surely there's hope!

Erica Jong

ERICA RAN INTO her editor's office and dropped a manuscript on his desk while he was on the phone. Then she fled New York City for a week.

"Anyway, I'm a poet," she consoled herself. "He'll hate my novel, but it won't make any difference. I'll just go on writing poetry."

The novel was *Fear of Flying*, which proceeded to fly off the best-seller charts. In short order, Erica Jong became one of the world's most widely acclaimed female novelists.

No one was more surprised than Erica. She knew the taboos of publishing. Serious women writers did not express sexual fantasies in "unladylike" language. Still, *Fear of Flying* was the book she had to get out of her system, and she was immensely relieved when it was finished. Already accepted as a first-rate poet, she could now return to writing slim volumes of poetry.

Fear of flying, writing, being read, living — where did it all come from?

As the daughter of affluent parents, Eda and Seymour Mann, she had been surrounded by good books, given art

73

Erica standing next to bulletin board

lessons, sent to summer camp. When Erica wrote a poem, her mother would suggest that she send it to the *New Yorker*.

"My parents were into education and self-improvement. They pushed me very hard," says Erica. "They were very positive toward me and thought I was wonderful and talented and beautiful. But at the same time there were a lot of negative things in my experience. My father was an importer who was away a lot, and my mother was a very troubled and frustrated person. I don't want to say critical things about her because I see how hard it was for her. She was a very creative and talented woman who had her own frustrations. She wasn't lucky enough to be born in an age where women could express themselves acceptably."

Everyday life made a greater impression on Erica than the advice that she send her poetry to the *New Yorker*. A fine artist, her mother set up her easel in the living room and fit her painting into a busy schedule of cooking, cleaning, and caring for three daughters. If guests were coming, the easel had to be put away. Yet her grandfather, who lived with them and was also an artist, enjoyed the large upstairs studio to himself, and her father was deferred to as head of the family during his brief visits home between business trips. It wasn't hard to determine who was important.

"Send it to the *New Yorker!*" There were no apparent limits to what Erica could aspire to, but her talented mother didn't rate her own studio. Confusing? Certainly.

"I was getting a mixed message that created a big stew of conflict," Erica explains. "Go out in the world and be who you are, my mom was saying, but at the same time the example she and other women set was that it's unfeminine to be too aggressive. I didn't know what to do. For a long time I did nothing. Oh, I wrote, but the thought of going public with my work frightened me. Part was fear of self-revelation, part female brainwashing which made it clear I shouldn't be assertive. Writing and publishing are, after all, aggressive, assertive acts."

The message a distinguished visiting critic gave her college English class was hardly mixed. "Women can't be writers," he railed. "They don't know blood and guts and puking in the streets and fucking whores. . ."

Erica remembers sadly the reaction of her intelligent Barnard classmates, some, like herself, aspiring writers. No one offered a word of protest. They all listened meekly to the authoritative male explain what women would not or could not write. As women, they were already well trained to accept the dashing of dreams. It was, after all, 1961. There weren't any women's studies courses, and there was no public women's movement. A woman's place? In the home.

Erica with her grandfather and her sister Susanna

Erica spent her school years identifying with writers and felt that the ones who really mattered were men. Even though she read women writers, they did not seem important. If they were good, she thought it was in spite of being female. If they were bad, it was because of it. She says she had "internalized all the dominant cultural stereotypes." As a result, she could hardly even imagine a woman as an author.

Since Erica believed no one would care about a woman's fate, she chose a male narrator for her first novel attempt. The first-person melodrama, about a young madman who thought he was God, fell apart after a hundred and fifty pages. Her next novel, written from the viewpoint of a male poet, died when she realized that the book was lifeless and, worse, that it was false. Neither effort saw print, but she learned a great deal from these aborted efforts.

From 1966 to 1969, Erica lived in Europe where her husband, a child psychiatrist, ran a guidance clinic for offspring of army personnel. The experience was a profoundly unhappy one but proved formative to her development as a writer. She felt alienated from the army people because she didn't believe in the Vietnam War, she was haunted by the idea of Hitler, and her marriage was floundering. To escape her misery, she immersed herself in the poetry of Sylvia Plath and Anne Sexton. Their example made it seem legitimate to express anger, to write about being a woman. Sonnets and sestinas about unicorns and the graves of English poets gave way to expressions of her innermost feelings in free verse. In her poetry, as well as in psychoanalysis, Erica began to deal with intensely negative feelings about being Jewish in Germany and with violent feelings about being a woman in a world dominated by men. "My poems," she says, "were frankly female, and for the first time being female became part of their subject."

This outpouring of emotion resulted in her best poetry yet, as she graduated from word play to her own authentic voice. Although her first poem had been published in *Epoch* magazine the year she graduated from college, for five years after that she found the idea of going public with her work overwhelming. In 1967, she resolved to end this silence and submit her poems for publication. Rejection slips did not stem the flow of words, but some caused so much pain that she delayed mailing out her poetry for months at a time. Gradually, the quality of her writing was reflected in sales to the *Beloit Poetry Journal* and *Mademoiselle*.

After three major rewrites, a collection of these poems titled *Fruits and Vegetables* was published by Holt, Rhinehart and Winston two years after her return to the United States. The book drew high critical praise and provided Erica one of the greatest thrills of her career. One reviewer called it a "dreamy yet graphic, seriously playful, wanton and earthy addition to the small stock of women poets who celebrate their sex."

Her editor, who had seen the beginning of her second novel attempt, urged her to abandon it and write the book he knew was in her, an authentic story told from a female viewpoint. Erica took his advice as a good sign. She had begun *Fear of Flying* the previous week. But she approached her fiction with trepidation, stopping frequently to write poetry. Finally, she put the novel aside to assemble the new poems and found she had a second book of poetry, *Half Lives*.

Erica describes herself at that stage as a closet fiction writer. She didn't dare show *Fear of Flying* to anyone. She worried that her agent and editor would think it far too sexually outspoken and concluded it was too literary to find a wide readership. But for the first time she was not evading herself. She wrote in her own voice, as if her life depended on it. To some extent, she felt it did.

Wanting to write female picaresque novels in the tradition of *Tom Jones, Augie March,* and Henry Miller's *Tropics*, Erica seized the same liberties with language male authors had long used. The eroticism accepted from Henry Miller and D. H. Lawrence had never before been accepted from a woman writer, and she knew it would meet the great resistance. Literary tradition notwithstanding, she decided to write the saga in her own style.

At least, she thought, even if unacceptable for publication, this novel will be authentic.

Isadora Wing, the heroine of *Fear of Flying*, and Erica Jong have much in common. Both were raised on New York's upper west side by well-to-do Jewish parents. Both excelled at New York's select High School of Music and Art, won honors at Barnard, married a college sweetheart who was felled by a nervous breakdown, divorced him, and then chose a Chinese-American psychiatrist as a second husband. Like Isadora, Erica is bright, witty, literate, and into psychoanalysis.

Many readers assume Isadora is Erica, and interviewers often ask the author just how autobiographical her books are. The public, having been titillated by Isadora's fantasies, is ravenous for gossip about Erica's personal life. As a result, she is one of the world's most interviewed people. At least it seems that way to her.

The assumption that she writes autobiography bothers her. She admits there's a lot of Erica in Isadora but explains she is a fiction writer. Many of the characters and events in her books are totally invented. Sometimes, she says, she can't even remember what actually happened and what didn't when she's finished writing. "Memory," she explains, "is neither literal nor factual; we rewrite the past as we live the present."

In *Fear of Flying*, she set out to write a satirical novel about a woman in search of her own identity and in the process mixed reality and fantasy as she pleased in hopes of elevating it to myth. Since few lives are well plotted, Erica sees the novelist's job as bringing form to experience. She says she writes about the world she knows because that enables her to chronicle life with a greater sense of immediacy. Other novelists before her—Defoe, Melville, Tolstoy, Colette, and Proust—did the same.

Erica standing, far right, with her parents and her sister Claudia

They, too, were once accused of writing autobiography, but because they are in the past, the gossip has long since died, and their works remain. "Someday," she declares, "I'll write a real autobiography, and then everyone will *really* be shocked."

For a long time, Erica wanted to follow family tradition and paint but later opted for writing since she felt there were too many painters in the family already. She wrote creatively throughout her childhood but not really seriously until she went to college in 1959. There she edited the college literary magazine, produced poetry programs for the campus radio station, and was elected to Phi Beta Kappa. She was known, she said, as the class grind because her classmates didn't realize that her idea of fun was studying English literature.

She describes her first husband, Michael Werthman, as her college sweetheart, best friend, and constant companion. But she says they were much too young and much too

Erica's high school yearbook photo

broke. After one and a half years of marriage, Michael's nervous breakdown detonated their relationship. The account of Isadora's first marriage in *Fear of Flying*, she says, comes closest to her real life.

After receiving her B.A. degree in 1963, Erica taught English at City College of New York. At the same time, she earned her M.A. degree in eighteenth-century literature. Graduate school and college teaching offered secur-

Erica in 1963 (photo by Bradford Backrach)

ity until, having almost completed her Ph.D., Erica was uprooted. She left to accompany her second husband, Dr. Allan Jong, who was drafted and sent to Germany.

Writing was a risky business; it never occurred to Erica that she could support herself doing it. Cut off from her studies and feeling totally miserable in a strange land, she was driven to express her feelings on paper. In poetry, she found she could deal freely with the most painful subjects. Her ability to create personae who spoke in her place protected her sense of privacy. Besides, she knew that even if her efforts were published, few people read poetry.

The good feelings that came with the publication of *Fruits and Vegetables* were to sustain her as her writing career careened roller coaster style after the acceptance of *Fear of Flying*. The problems began before the book saw print when the original typesetter objected to the language and refused to work on it. Some reviewers were extremely hostile. In the *New Statesman*, a critic described the "witless heroine" of "this crappy novel" as a "mammoth pudenda."

Not all the reviews were attacks. John Updike gave Erica her finest moment since publication of her first book of poetry when he said *Fear of Flying* has "class, sass, brightness and bite" and "looks like a winner." Henry Miller wrote, "In many ways she is more forthright, more honest, more daring than most male authors . . . I feel like predicting that this book will make literary history, that because of it women are going to find their own voice and give us great sagas of sex, life, joy and adventure."

Despite its critics, *Fear of Flying* did go on to make literary history. The hard-cover book was a sellout, and a year later the paperback edition took off like a rocket. It spent months on the best-seller lists. At last count, twenty-five foreign editions of the book had been issued, and it was in its forty-fifth printing, having sold over 6 million copies.

Erica, who thought of herself primarily as a poet, was catapulted on to center state. Fame and fortune were heaped at her doorstep, finally broke down the door, and all but annihilated the small blonde woman on the other side.

She was not prepared for the virulent reactions her novel evoked. The publication of *Fear of Flying* brought her face to face with the double standard for male and female authors. She discovered what was "candid" coming from a male author was considered "whiny" when it came from a female. She says that nothing in her life prepared her for "the outraged puritanism which reduced Isadora Wing to a sort of Happy Hooker and saw nothing in the book but sex, sex, sex!"

Suddenly, she was a public personality, a cult figure who appeared on talk shows from coast to coast, lectured at college campuses, and tried to deal with men who thought Erica was Isadora Wing whose one overwhelming wish was for sex.

The pressures on her were enormous. Her marriage to Allan Jong was giving the final death rattle. As a "public property," she found the demands on her time incessant. She wanted to respond to her readers who wrote voluminous letters about their problems, but the mail came in great bags. The task was hopeless. She was trying to write her second novel and promote her first one at the same time. Many men were threatened by her outspoken views on equality of the sexes. Yet feminists accused her of copping out for her heroine's preoccupation with men.

So this was fame. Erica candidly admits she had sought it, worked long and hard in its pursuit. When most of her classmates at college were having babies, she was certain she had to establish herself as a writer before she even considered the possibility of children. Her need for a career became an obsession. The example of her mother's conflict between obligations to her family and her passion for painting did not encourage compromise. Erica vowed not to be frustrated in the same way.

Looking back on her struggles to maintain equilibrium when her world seemed to be disintegrating, Erica says, "I think God gave me a lesson in giving me fame because I wanted it very badly and saw none of the negative parts of it. I had to have it and see some of the bad things about it in order to be taught to be more inner-directed. Fame means millions of people have a wrong idea of who you are. They imagine you to be all kinds of erroneous things.

That forces you to center yourself, to find out who you are and to develop a bit of independence from public judgment. It's hard, very hard, and very strange and very good. People who don't have it think fame makes you arrogant. It doesn't. If you use it as a tool of self-awareness, it's extremely humbling."

Erica was eventually able to look back on her year of self-exposure and see it as a learning experience. Although she was temporarily thrown into depression (she gained twenty pounds and cut off her hair), she emerged knowing she was much more resilient than she had ever suspected. She began to realize that achieving success wasn't going to solve her personal problems. Erica describes that realization as her first step toward enlightenment.

One thing *Fear of Flying* did for Erica was to make her more and more aware of how empty life was lived in public and on paper. She needed loving relationships. Her marriage to Allan Jong could scarcely be classified as loving, yet it was difficult to end. Admitting failure for the second time was emotionally excruciating.

Reflecting on her reasons for marrying Jong, Erica says when her first marriage dissolved, she was looking for stability above all else. She chose a man she describes as "very dour and kind of strict. . .a kind of daddy." Although she says they never laughed together, she thought that as a wife of a psychiatrist she would be "taken care of." He would, she hoped, help her conquer her many fears. She was also aware that his financial support would buy her time to write. Writing, she rationalized, was more important than romantic happiness. Had he said she could no longer write, Erica declares she would have left instantly.

Erica remained faithful to Jong for years and maintained the relationship far longer than was good for her emotional well-being. The divorce was incredibly difficult because her husband and his lawyer concluded she was wealthy. She admits the timing was bad. Possibly the worst year to get divorced, she reflected, is the one in which you become famous.

During the enormous success of *Fear of Flying* and the final dissolution of her marriage, Erica felt pulled apart by her need for a career and her need for a fulfilling personal life. She says that she always felt that being a woman writer meant giving up what other people have: marriage, children, and a family life. Her whole orientation to being female was that you had to pay for the privilege.

She remembers being warned that if she got a doctorate she probably would never find a husband. Would she have to hide her competence so men would not feel envious or threatened? Half of Erica was the artist who loved to write and wanted success. The other half was the nice little girl who needed approval and knew that to get it she should do what society expected. It did not seem possible to be strong and determined and still be feminine and loved.

It wasn't fair. Men did not have to choose between work and love. They could have both. But the women she knew who were mothers usually received so little help from their husbands that they had to give up the idea of a career at least while their children were small. They had no supportive spouses at home to cook and clean and bring up the children so that they were free to concentrate on their work.

She was all too familiar with the traditional idea of marriage, which she describes as a master-servant relationship. Women were expected to submerge their own identities, to see themselves as helpers rather than separate beings. This is tragic for a writer who cannot contribute anything original until she has an authentic sense of self and has learned to trust her own voice.

But she did want someone to share love and sex with. Erica doesn't understand why being a feminist should be inconsistent with loving men. Her sense of joy comes from having love in her life. She knows she can live without it but really doesn't want to.

After two broken marriages, Erica was keenly aware of the fact that matrimony does not come with any lifetime guarantees. A license or a vow doesn't automatically make someone loyal. It certainly wouldn't protect her from being betrayed sexually or emotionally.

Her second novel, *How To Save Your Own Life*, dealt with the dual problems of establishing a satisfying personal life after a painful divorce and coping with fame. At the end of *Fear of Flying*, which Erica describes as a story of adolescent rebellion, the reader has to guess what the heroine's next move might be. Erica says that she wanted to show that such a woman could move on into a good relationship with men, that it was not impossible for her.

Just as in her first novel, there are many parallels to Erica's life in *How To Save Your Own Life*. Isadora goes on to try to cope with fame from her best seller *Candida Confesses*, while Jong tried to cope with the problems brought on by *Fear of Flying*'s runaway success. Both heroine and author end up loving a younger bearded man from California, Josh in the novel, Jonathan Fast in real life. (It is one of the ironies of their present life that though Jon is in reality from New York, everyone insists to his face that he must be from California because his fictional alter ego is a native Californian. Apparently, fiction speaks louder than fact.) Isadora Wing overcomes irrational fears, seizes her own life, and begins to make choices based on self-acceptance and a sense of joy.

To people who say "I know Isadora is really you," Erica answers, "I wish she were. I'm not as brave." Besides, the only relevant questions as far as the novelist is concerned are "Does the book move you? Does it make you think?"

Erica was pleased with *How To Save Your Own Life*. She felt it was a better crafted book than *Fear of Flying*, that it showed a greater degree of professionalism. However, it did not come easily. In fact, she described writing a second novel after a big success as the hardest thing she had ever done. "No matter what I wrote after *Fear of Flying*, it would be cannon fodder. So how are you going to deal with this?" she asks. "You can stop writing for twelve years like Joseph Heller and waste twelve years of your life, but it's the only life you have. There aren't a lot of twelve-year periods in it to work, so you go upstairs and write. My worst fears about the reception of *How To Save Your Own Life* were realized. In fact, it was worse than I could have ever imagined. I'm not a splenetic person, and I can't even imagine all the nasty things people will think of. I couldn't even think of some of the character assassinations that came after its publication."

Success, Erica found, did have its positive aspects. Along with the criticism came money. And money meant freedom. She was no longer economically dependent on a man. She would not have to write ad copy or mark freshman themes to make a living. In fact, she was a forerunner in a rather recent trend in this country in which women have become increasingly independent economically. Erica says this puts them in the position to choose men for companionship and love rather than out of desperate need for social status and financial support. She considers the greatest freedom in the world is to love without any consideration of what a man can offer in terms of material goods.

Just as in the end of *How To Save Your Own Life* Isadora finds a man who needs her as much as she needs him, Erica found Jon. She says that not until she was thirty-two did she find someone as interesting to her as her work. At twenty-nine, Jon was not as hung up about women as older men she knew. He didn't have to dominate or make more money than she did in order to prove his manhood. He didn't feel threatened helping with domestic chores. She had found a man who filled her need for a companionable friends-and-lovers kind of relationship.

Finally, she had equal measures of love and work in her life without assuming a subservient role. She says, "Only after I became a success in my profession and started making a lot of money and started to feel myself to be important in the world of men could I have a relationship with a man like this one. It took being a success in the big world to come back to my home."

Once having believed that misery was an automatic byproduct when a woman becomes a professional writer, she now knew joy. It seemed to her entirely possible to have love and tenderness without giving up freedom, creativity, and independence. She finds it not at all surprising that some of the most ardent feminists have also been the most passionate writers about love.

Since Erica was disillusioned with marriage as an institution, she chose instead to live with Jon. Sometimes when she read a terrible review of one of her books, she would get a sudden urge to exchange vows. But Jon would gently point out that a matrimonial contract would not stop bad reviews.

Despite a lack of formal declaration of their love, they gradually became more and more committed. "We've only been together for four years," says Erica, "and we've been very monogamous. We've only had one or two occasions where we weren't, but that was in the beginning of our relationship. We told each other and talked about it, and there wasn't a serious major jealousy. As we get tighter and tighter as a couple, it would be harder and harder. At the moment, it doesn't seem like a problem. We're not itchy. We've talked about the fact that if either of us ever felt that itchiness, we would rather deal with it in some way together than deal with it with an affair that might split the basic dyad. I think an affair is destructive, and I don't know many couples that have survived it."

While Erica and Jon did not "believe" in marriage, they did believe in their relationship and worked hard to keep the lines of communication open. Also, they both wanted children. After trying for a long time to become pregnant, Erica told Jon, "Maybe I feel sort of insecure because we're not married. Maybe my subconscious is that bourgeois." Although it defied their principles, they bought a marriage license. At first, they didn't use it; they had too many ambivalent feelings about legalizing their love. But Jon felt they might as well marry since they were going to be together the rest of their lives, anyway. Also, he saw far too many legal difficulties in store for an illegitimate child.

A week after the wedding, the doctor confirmed the couple's suspicion that they were going to have a baby. Erica feels just having the license helped her conceive.

During her pregnancy, Erica had amniocentesis, a test for abnormalities in which amniotic fluid is drawn from the womb. When the doctor told her the baby was female, Erica felt depressed. She was in the middle of a book tour, being constantly confronted with reactionary attitudes toward sex roles. "I was filled with sadness," she says, "that she would have to grow up in a country where the attitude toward women is so stereotypical and prejudiced."

In an article for *Ladies Home Journal*, she articulated her hopes and fears for her unborn daughter. Erica wrote that she hoped her child would grow up to find the choices not quite as harsh as the ones she had faced. She wanted her daughter to be both loving and competent in her work without feeling torn between the two. She wished she could live in a world in which men aren't threatened by women of achievement, one in which the pleasures and duties of parenthood are more equally shared by men and women.

Erica sees the problems between mothers and daughters as far more complex than those between mothers and sons partly because women's concepts of themselves are undergoing such drastic changes. She feels they are able to give their sons unambivalent affection, but their relationship with their daughters is complicated because mothers are so intent on undoing the mistakes their mothers made. The daughter usually ends up with less unequivocal approval than the son. As a result, girls tend to be less secure and therefore quicker to abandon personal needs of achievement in order to win the love of a man.

Erica says her pregnancy was "great and wonderful and healthy." "I looked radiant and felt terrific," she enthuses. "I did yoga into my seventh month, and my yoga teacher, my doctor, everybody said the baby's going to pop out with no trouble. But it didn't happen as everyone predicted. The labor was not short, it was difficult. The baby's head was turned, so it was too big for my pelvis, and I had to have a cesarean. I recovered very fast, and the cutting was neatly done, so I don't have horrible scars, but it was a profoundly shocking experience. I came out of it amazed that the human race has survived. I think that women who have had many children are absolutely heroic. I emerged with a tremendous sense of affirmation about being a woman."

Erica now looks forward to the challenge of rearing her daughter, Molly Miranda. She wants her baby to grow up with positive feelings toward herself and her sexuality. "I feel very blessed," she says, "that I didn't have a baby with Allan Jong, because our relationship was so troubled. There was a time when our marriage was really flying apart, and we kept saying we should have a baby to patch it up, which is the dumbest thing. I have faith that Jon

Erica and her daughter Molly Miranda, 1978
(photo by Bill Gleasner)

and I have a very positive relationship and that Molly will
get that by osmosis. I guess if the parents love each other
and are demonstrative and affectionate and pretty open
about sex, you've got to trust that that gets transmitted."

Since very few women her age had mothers who had
successfully resolved the dilemma of work and love, Erica
is trying hard to pass a positive example along to her
daughter. "To my child," she says, "it will seem like the
way of the world to have a mother who spends at least
four hours a day at the typewriter." She hopes to provide
a role model who has equal parts of love and work in her
life, who never sacrifices one for the other.

Since Erica can afford a full-time nurse for the baby,
she realizes her situation is not typical. She also knows her
ability to have a full-time career and be a good mother
may create conflicts in the future. "It's easier now," she
says. "I open my blouse and breast-feed her, but she's not
asking me questions about the universe. I know that men
don't feel as much guilt. That's where my views on this
matter have sort of changed. After carrying the baby,
you're linked. That's not to say that men don't love their
children. They can be enormously concerned, but there's
much more visceral link from the mother to the child,
which puts the greater burden on the woman."

Despite this added responsibility, Erica has not slack-
ened her writing pace. "I work like a demon," she says.
"You need stamina, more energy than anyone ever
thinks. I drive myself to sit down at my desk on days when
I'm exhausted. Even on days when the baby's been up
twice at night and I've gotten up at six o'clock to breast-
feed, I force myself to work. I know I have a block of four
hours to work, and, by God, I'm going to use it. I'm
amazed how driven I am.

"There are a lot of things that drive me, but one is that
this book is an immense challenge because I've forced myself to write a book in the voice of an eighteenth-century
woman. She's a lot like me in many ways, but in other
ways she's different. I want to prove to myself that I can
do it. Once you've started a book, you want to push yourself to the limit and go beyond what you know you can do.
Also, you want each book to be better than the last."

Research has proved time consuming. "My secretary,"
she says, "runs to the library and pulls out billions of
books and orders microfilms, but of course I have to read
everything. I've read so many books for this book that if I
wanted to put a bibliography on it, I wouldn't be able to
fit them all in. For example, my heroine just had a baby,
and I just had a baby. But having a baby in 1724 is not
like having a baby in 1978. I had to read the history of ob-
stetrics and midwifery. Then I had to decide for the good
of the plot how she is going to have this baby, who would
deliver her, what complications she would suffer. (She
can't die in childbirth because she's writing her memoirs
at the age of forty-seven.)"

Erica used to claim she would stop writing novels if she
ever had enough money to support her poetry habit, but
she's changed. She's convinced poetry and fiction use different parts of her brain, consume different kinds of
energy. "Spiritually, I'm a poet," she says. "That's where

I started, and I feel even my novels come out of a poet's sensibility. But I've gotten hooked on writing novels, and I enjoy it. Novel writing is the most fascinating process of self-discovery in the world. You discover ideas you never knew you had and characters you never knew you knew. In a novel, you can deal with the social fabric and the way people interact in families and the way society impinges on the individual. You can't do that in a poem, certainly not to the same extent. A poem is an individual insight. I always write poems while I'm writing novels. I think that probably for the rest of my life I'll do both. I don't feel they're mutually exclusive."

Writing is not easy for Erica, but when she's working, she's happy. She's able to conquer her persistent feelings of anticipatory dread and exist entirely in the present. Sometimes the words seem to come almost as if by divine dictation. She says, "If I've done my two or three pages (which is my output when I'm working on a novel), I know that I'll feel good the rest of the day. Whatever else I do, whether it's grocery shopping with Jon, taking care of the baby or going out to dinner with friends, I'll feel wonderful. I've had my fix for the day."

"Writing is a kind of meditation for me. It centers me. It keeps me from flying off at loose ends. Each day that I don't write I get more fragmented. Even on vacation I write. If I'm working on a novel, and we go away, I try to leave the whole thing behind, but I bring my notebook. I always write poetry because that to me is my euphoria. My mind is soothed by writing, both poetry and novels. I can't *not write*. I can *not publish*, but I can't *not write*."

Erica has certainly considered the possibility of withholding her work from publication. If she did, she would be spared "flack from the literary establishment," the attacks that cause her so much pain. She says that it's tough to be a writer, tougher to be a woman, and toughest of all to be a woman writer. "I'm a little pessimistic about the future of the woman writer," she admits, "because it seems to me that writers who dare to question the way society is established get a lot of grief in their own life. When I look back on the reviews that women writers like Charlotte Brontë got in the nineteenth century, they are not so different from the ones that are gotten by revolutionary women writers of today. What we tend to see is that women writers who are nonthreatening, who don't really rock the boat, and who are very good in terms of writing nice prose tend to get praised, whereas the ones who are really questioning the fabric of society don't. *Fear of Flying* upset the critics at least partly because in it a woman has an adulterous affair and does not die. So in a way it shatters an archetype."

She's found that women who review women are more hostile than men because "they're token women in a male preserve. If you've ever been the only woman on a committee of men, the way you behave is very funny. You don't want to be harsh and castrating. You want to show that you're a very reasonable and rational person. You behave differently than if it were half men and half women. The token woman syndrome is very strange. Women bend over backwards to show that they're fair and not favoring their own sex. Men have no problem with favoring their own sex."

Erica has definite feelings about token woman tactics. "I will not," she says, "because I've been pilloried, pillory other writers. I don't want to become like the people who feed off me. I don't want the bad karma that it will bring."

Her advice to young people who aspire to the life of the professional writer is to read and write. "Read every book you can get your hands on," she says. "Read what you love. Write constantly. Write journals, poems, anything. Study the style of writers you love because basically writers teach themselves to write. Go to writing workshops if you must but don't listen terribly hard to what people say, especially if they're discouraging. Don't trust rejection slips because they mean nothing. Keep writing. Never give up."

Rejection still bothers Erica. Not rejection in the form of printed slips from editors but rejection from the critics who review her work. Their hostility has made her self-conscious and threatens the very candor that has made her books meaningful to a large segment of the populace. She's tried very hard for honesty in her life and admits the whole situation is upsetting. "There's been such an attempt in some quarters to silence me," she says. "I have to fight it a lot. That frightens me, especially when I realize that every book I send out to the world is going to face this barrage before it reaches its natural audience."

She says, "My books have all had a kind of word-of-mouth success. Success has never come from the establishment. It's always come from the readers. I want to be honest, to use my heart as a kind of laboratory where I can find out what others are thinking. As a writer, I have an obligation to write what I feel."

Many people write to verify that Erica is very much on track. They send long, intelligent, passionate letters to tell her they are reading the truth about what women feel for the first time. They are less lonely knowing others experience the same emotions. "My fans," says Erica, "understand me better than the critics."

The only way Erica can preserve her candor is to pretend her work will never be published. "I try not to think about publication," she says. "When I started this novel, I didn't sign it up on the basis of an outline. I wrote a hundred and seventy pages before I even showed it to the publisher." This way she is able to write for herself rather than to please an imaginary audience. She kept telling herself she was fooling around. She researched for a year and wrote for a year. After she had submitted her work, she thought she was too far into it not to finish the book. "That gave me considerable freedom," she says.

In order to grow as a writer, Erica tries new forms of expression from time to time. She's written a book of essays that she's very pleased with. But again the hostility she's sure is waiting troubles her. "I'm very afraid to publish these essays because they're very incendiary and tremendously feminist," she says. "The feminist establishment writers say, 'Oh, she's not a feminist,' and the male critics say, 'She's an incorrigible man hater,' so I fall into the middle where I get attacked from both sides."

She says, "I think the stresses success brings are absolutely mind boggling, and I don't think anyone ever knows who hasn't been through it because you have to deal with hate. With success comes enormous envy from others, negative vibes that are coming at me all the time. Women aren't able to cope well with that. We are so trained to need approval. We need too much to be loved."

"I think," she says thoughtfully, "what I've gotten out of all this is that one cannot live by other's opinions of you. If I could go back and change one thing in my life, I would be more independent, more inner-directed."

In spite of all the hostility she's had to absorb, Erica feels it's vital for other women to see a female author who doesn't give up, go insane, or stick her head in the oven like Sylvia Plath. The best example she can set is to go on writing, to produce lots of books, and to be a rational spokeswoman for her ideas.

To accomplish this, she knows she has to take risks, to challenge the unknown, to do the things she fears the most. "No one," she says, "avoids being a fool without also avoiding growth."

Erica Jong is committed to flying — on her own slightly frayed but very strong wings.

Jessamyn West

J ESSAMYN LOOKED at the blood she had coughed up. More trouble. Hadn't she had enough problems with her health?

For a year, she had been dragging herself around. It had been difficult coping with the heavy load of studies required of a Ph.D. candidate. Keeping her mind on the great literature of the world when she was always coughing and often feverish was impossible.

Her husband urged her again and again to go to the university infirmary. She approached each visit with renewed hope. Maybe her problem would finally be diagnosed and a cure found. First, they had treated her for an ordinary tooth infection. Later, they explored the possibility of an exotic tropical fever. When the TB patch test showed her free of the dreaded lung disease, the doctor suggested she was suffering from anxiety. Certainly anyone preparing for final exams was a little nervous.

Luckily, she was home for a visit when she coughed up the blood. Her mother whisked her to the family doctor who x-rayed her lungs and diagnosed an advanced case of

99

Jessamyn West (photo by Bill Gleasner)

tuberculosis. Her body, already at war against the tuber-
cle bacilli, had ignored the patch test, which consisted of
a mere pinprick of bacilli.

The sentence (no one called it a cure): at least two
years' bed rest in a sanatorium. So much for her studies.
"One cup of blood," she said, "separated me from being a
Ph.D. candidate and made me a certified TB-er."

Jessamyn was afraid to ask the doctor if she were dying.
After all, she was only twenty-nine. His "encouragement"
consisted of reminding her that many invalids had not
given up their work. He mentioned the poet John Keats,
Chopin, the great composer, and Farrell Loomis, a lawyer who had saved a local bank $50,000 after he'd lost a
lung. Unfortunately, Jessamyn knew Keats had died at
twenty-five and Chopin in his thirties. Loomis had been
buried a few days before.

Yet not all the Farrell Loomises in the world could
dampen her joy. At last her problem had been identified.
After two years of afternoon fevers, gasping for breath
after climbing stairs, and crawling to the bathroom with
pleurisy pains, she knew her illness was real. She was not a
hypochondriac, after all. Jessamyn felt that she had been
pulled back from the brink of insanity.

Being placed in a sanatorium terminal ward quickly
dispelled her elation. Because she had hemorrhaged, her
case was considered far advanced. The booklet she was
handed, titled "What You Need to Know About Tuberculosis," was of very little comfort. It included the grim
statistic that 95 percent of those who enter a sanatorium
with "far advanced" TB are dead within five years.

The sanatorium doctor was hardly more encouraging.
His first words were, "Not very emaciated yet, are we,
Mrs. McPherson?" It was a prophecy, not a question.
Turning for cheer to fellow patients was futile. Terminal
warders were engaged in an all-out battle for survival.

Every ounce of energy was used to cough or simply to breathe. Morning would often reveal an empty bed, the mattress airing on the outside railing.

Jessamyn knew the empty bed meant another death, but she had no intention of dying. Her mother, furious with the idea of her daughter in a terminal ward, had her moved to a different section. She shared Jessamyn's conviction that she would eventually leave the sanatorium—on her feet.

It soon became apparent that Jessamyn was not a candidate for a quick cure. She suffered with night sweats, a rasping cough, and raging fevers. In 1931, treatment for tuberculosis consisted almost entirely of bed rest and overeating. Her life revolved around a relentless schedule of temperature taking and weighing. Jessamyn could not control her fever, but weight was another thing. Bland institutional food and lack of appetite were not going to cause her to lose ground. She simply added tubes of toothpaste and jars of cold cream to her bathrobe pockets. It was the only way she knew to keep the scales from accurately reflecting her condition. "This," she remembers, "necessitated additional weights each weighing day until finally I clanked on to the scales as lumpy and burdened as a pack mule."

Convinced her cure lay in following every rule, she ate all her food, drank eight glasses of water a day, and breathed carefully from the stomach. She never laughed after being warned that laughing might break open a lesion in her lungs causing another hemorrhage. But instead of improving, she became steadily worse.

As her misery intensified, she planned her escape. Guns, drugs, and razor blades were not available. Hanging required more strength than she possessed. Electrocution was the only possible answer. She would crawl to the bathroom, fill the tub, turn on the heater, get into the water, and pull the heater in with her. All her suffering would be over! What a relief it was to have a plan.

Whenever she felt she had the energy to carry it off, someone was in the bathroom. Gradually, she weakened to the point where she could not even crawl. After two years of treatment, the doctor asked her parents to take their daughter home to die among loved ones. The sanatorium considered her case hopeless, and by this time Jessamyn agreed. She wanted nothing more than to die. In fact, she cried every morning on finding herself still alive. But her mother refused to give up. She plied Jessamyn with orange juice mixed with raw eggs, gave her a kitten, and entertained her with turn-of-the-century tales of her childhood in Indiana.

Her temperature began to drop, and she gained weight. Jessamyn started reading again, although she only had strength for a paragraph or two at a time. When the doctor pronounced her well enough to endure the twenty-mile ride to his office for an x-ray, her mother bought her a new outfit. Jessamyn put on the clothes but thought she looked ridiculous in the hat. She promptly kicked it under the bed.

Her mother remembered the incident as a triumph. Up to that time, Jessamyn had been totally without spunk. She had eaten whatever she was served and never seemed to care what she looked like. Her mother was relieved to see the first glimmer of Jessamyn's once-lively personality return. She told her daughter that the moment she kicked the hat under the bed she knew the battle was won.

When one of her visitors suggested she sew a quilt for her mother to remember her by, Jessamyn decided to pick up her pen. Needlework wasn't the only thing that could be done in bed.

Jessamyn realized later that the doctorate in English literature, which had almost been hers, had been her way of

*Jessamyn, beginning to be able to sit up to write after
her bout with tuberculosis*

staying as close to writing as possible. She says she was not
proud of the way she became a writer, unable to do anything else after being cornered by her illness. While talent
may be helpful, she says a writer's sine qua non is guts.
They give the first push that eventually uncovers the
talent.

Her love of words, books, and writing did not begin in
the boredom of the sick bed. At three, Jessamyn had sat
sobbing in the corner because she could not make sense of

Writing in bed while recovering

the words in the book she held. By the time she was twelve, she had read almost all the books in her home. Just in time, a library came into her life. It didn't matter that it consisted of about fifty books in a reconditioned janitor's closet in the local school. She says that her adult intellectual life began the summer evening she asked her father for a silver dollar to buy a library card.

At fourteen, she began a scrapbook full of lists of words and sample plots. But she never thought of telling anyone about it. If a child has dancing or musical talent, she says, he is usually encouraged and given special lessons. But someone who likes to read and write "needs a vein of iron to keep at it."

She thought of writing as a presumptuous act and was convinced that she must be given some sign that would indicate she should be a writer. A penetrating look in her mirror revealed nothing but freckles. The beginning of writing for her was not telling anyone of her passion for words. She had never seen a writer, never knew anyone else who had seen one. Writers certainly couldn't be ordinary mortals. It was an enormous revelation to her when she later discovered writers were just human beings who wrote.

As the long backed-up desire to write was released, words flowed. Visitors seeing her cheerfully engrossed approved. At last, Jessamyn could rationalize what she most wanted to do.

Writing about her life as an invalid was too depressing. The future was, at best, uncertain. Jessamyn chose her first subject matter from the tales her mother had told during her recuperation. Stories of Grace West's childhood among the Quakers created a whole new world that helped her escape the daily misery of illness. She lived nearer the land of her mother's girlhood than to anything in her own state of California.

Even after returning to live with her husband, Jessamyn continued the limited existence of an invalid. She had learned the lesson of her frailty well. Once before, she had attempted to resume a normal life with him only to end up back in the sanatorium. It would never happen again. The terrors of the terminal ward were branded on her brain.

There was ample time to assess the damage. She says that in the struggle she lost the confidence and resilience of youth along with the ability to ever again live a life that was not introspective.

Sickness had made it possible for her to write without appearing pretentious, but submitting her work for publication was another matter altogether. It struck her as immodest to act as if her work could possibly be worthy of publication.

Her husband did not share her timidity and urged her to submit her stories to magazines. Gradually, he was able to convince her that the presumption would be on the part of the editors. After all, they were the ones to decide what was publishable. Finally, she realized he would persist until she proved him wrong. She agreed to send out some stories on the condition that once they had all been rejected, he would stop mentioning it. Max's idea proved valid. The McPhersons celebrated the publication of Jessamyn's first story in 1939.

She chose her markets carefully. By sending her stories to literary magazines that paid little or nothing, she was able to save herself an "enormous number of refusals." It was a time of high excitement. The professors who edited the literary magazines wrote to her. She had never saved a letter from a boy friend, but the first one she received from an editor was placed under her pillow so she could wake up at night and read it again.

Writing for money never occurred to her. Since Max was employed as a teacher, she knew she was going to eat whether anything was accepted for publication or not. Nevertheless, she was thrilled to receive her first check from a little magazine called *Foothills*. Its editors had published several of her stories without pay but at the end of the year awarded her a five-dollar prize for the magazine's best published story.

Having her work accepted fanned the creative flame in her. She worked steadily, gradually learning to cope with the inevitable rejections. "I'm mulish," she says. "When I'd get a rejection for a story, I would think, *This will not be the end of this!*" Persistence paid off, and soon she had a sizable group of stories in print.

Jessamyn was delighted when Harcourt Brace agreed to publish a collection of the Quaker stories set in Indiana. *The Friendly Persuasion*, published in 1945 when she was forty-three, was an immediate success. The book earned almost unanimous critical acclaim, made money, and sold to the movies. Jessamyn acknowledges that these events would have been high points to anyone who knew anything about writing, but she had no idea at the time how unusual this success was.

Just after the book's publication, the publisher invited her to come to New York for two weeks. All the way from California? She thought the idea nonsensical, even dangerous. Now that she had finally started writing, she reasoned she should stay at home and write. So much valuable time had already been lost. Besides, she was still recuperating and needed rest. She was convinced she would collapse at an interview and expire if she had to meet a live editor.

Mrs. West had different ideas. She told Jessamyn that by being fearful of everything, she was living as if she were already dead. Her mother urged her to go because she said they might never ask her again.

Later, Jessamyn realized her mental state was that of an invalid who had been institutionalized for too long. New York turned out to be a peak experience. The people she had feared turned out to be kindred souls who shared her enthusiasm for books and writing. Editors proved to be human beings. Cocktail parties failed to do her in. She survived without her daily rest period, and she completely forgot to take her temperature.

Harcourt Brace was so enthusiastic about the reception of *The Friendly Persuasion* they asked her to write a novel. Jessamyn knew that novels had a reputation for selling better than short-story collections and agreed to try, but she suffered with the idea. It seemed like such a complex and difficult task. At first, she approached each chapter as if it had to be resolved like a separate story but soon saw that wouldn't work. Writing *The Witch Diggers* was a struggle, but when she completed the book, she realized that novels were really easier than stories.

Although Jessamyn still feels weak as a plotter, she says that a novel doesn't demand nearly as tight a construction as a story. You simply live with the characters for a considerable length of time and write things as they happen. But a short story, like a poem, she feels, must be convoluted for a purpose.

The new insight did not diminish her love of writing short stories. She had become a master of the form, and her output was prodigious. The success of *The Friendly Persuasion* had added an agent to her life, one who was not content with the idea of selling work to literary magazines for little or no pay. One of his first actions on her behalf was to sell several stories to the *Ladies Home Journal*. The pay was greater than any she'd ever received for one of her stories, but Jessamyn was disgusted by the idea of being a ladies' magazine writer. She immediately wrote three stories as unlike the ladies' market as anything she'd ever seen. "Henry," she wrote, "here are three stories which I defy you to sell to the *Ladies Home Journal*." He answered that she had sent him three stories that he didn't think he could sell to anyone. Yet one of them was placed immediately with the prestigious *New Yorker* magazine. Jessamyn laughs, remembering her "snobbish" attitude. "It was the first time in my life I ever slanted a story," she says, "and the slant was *away* from the *Ladies Home Journal*."

Although she wrote on a wide variety of themes, it was for her Quaker stories that Jessamyn West was best known. She resented being typecast as a Quaker and lived to regret the fact that *The Friendly Persuasion* had been her first book. "There are people who liked *The Friendly Persuasion*," she says. "They want me to write about sweet Quakers the rest of my life. There are people who never liked the sweet Quakers in the beginning, and they don't read anything I write because they think it's all going to be about sweet Quakers. I fall between the two."

The Witch Diggers, published in 1951, was set in southern Indiana, just as *The Friendly Persuasion* had been. Yet the approach was far different. Most readers assumed her collection of stories was based on fact, whereas the novel was imagined. Jessamyn says the truth is just the opposite, that *The Witch Diggers* was far closer to reality. She said, "*The Friendly Persuasion* is not nostalgic, as has been said, since it does not report anything I remember. It is utopian (in as far as I'm concerned) in that it creates an imagined (and to me) pleasant world. *Witch Diggers* is the world I know."

She wrote it "to become an honest woman." She felt that *The Friendly Persuasion* told of a very small segment of people in southern Indiana who were unusually blessed. She said she did not feel she had told the truth either about people or herself until she had written of less fortunate people. "Now," she wrote, "I feel pen-wise, an honest woman, and can just write a book next time and not be bothered with past accounts."

Being an honest woman is a high priority with Jessamyn West. Her philosophy of writing is summed up in her statement: "He who cares more for what is good than what is true loses, in the long run, both goodness and truth. For without truth there is no goodness." She feels it is wrong to keep books from young people that contain "ugly truths" while letting them read ones with "pretty lies." The only kind of dirty book, she says, is one that falsifies life. She felt far less damaged by reading about brutal truths than by sentimental misrepresentations of human relationships.

Although Jessamyn was born in Indiana, most of her childhood memories are of southern California. She was just six when her parents, Eldo and Grace West, built a house on the barren land they later turned into a citrus

The West children in Jennings County, Indiana; Jessamyn, front left

grove. Roaming the desert and nearby cactus-covered foothills, the four West children quickly learned to love their new home. For Jessamyn, the wild, spare and tawny became the standard of beauty by which she would judge all scenery the rest of her life.

Jessamyn's horizons expanded when she commuted from Yorba Linda to high school in Fullerton and later

Jessamyn as a high school senior, age sixteen

entered Whittier College. At Whittier, a small Quaker institution, she participated in sports, debating, and the
literary society. She also became engaged to a handsome
student, Harry Maxwell McPherson.

The dean of women cautioned her that if she and Max
continued seeing so much of each other, "the association
will lead to marriage." Since that was Jessamyn's firm

Jessamyn at nineteen

resolve, she was glad that the dean concurred and couldn't imagine what she was being warned about. Her entire sex education received at home consisted of a stern admonition not to talk about it. Looking back, Jessamyn wonders why she had so little curiosity. She relished the idea of sex as mystery and didn't want to be confused with facts. Certainly, the little talk the local minister's wife gave to the engaged girls in college did absolutely nothing to enlighten her. The Roaring Twenties, she observed, never did roar for her.

After a Quaker wedding, the young couple moved to Hemet, California, where Jessamyn taught in a one-room schoolhouse. Although she thoroughly enjoyed teaching all six grades, after four years, she decided it was time to further her own education. She spent the summer of 1929 at Oxford University in England and then rejoined her husband at the University of California at Berkeley. There she was given her first encouragement as a writer. She was totally stunned when, after reading her research paper aloud, her favorite English professor said, "I don't know whether you realize how wonderful this is or not."

The lung hemorrhage, which brought her studies to an abrupt halt, was not quite the tragedy that it seemed. At the time, she thought it was the lowest point in her life. "I thought my life was over," she says. "As it turned out, actually it was one of the highest points. Except for the lung trouble, I would have gone on and been a professor. I'm not going to say 'God bless tuberculosis,' but without that I think I might never have written."

In 1953, Harcourt Brace published Jessamyn's fourth book, *Cress Delahanty*, a collection of stories about a young girl growing up in California. Since the time and setting of the book correspond to Jessamyn's childhood, she finally was able to break away from being labeled solely as a Quaker writer. She believed that life was inextricably mixed and wanted to write it that way. She thought she knew quite a bit more than just about the life of Quakers in Indiana a hundred years ago.

Certainly she knew something about her main character, Cress, a sensitive girl with literary leanings whose father was a citrus grower. *Cress Delahanty* was well

reviewed and was chosen as a Book of the Month Club se-
lection. Although fiction, the book rang true to the emotional turmoil that many girls go through growing up.

Jessamyn's experience working on the movie script for
The Friendly Persuasion was recorded in her first book of
nonfiction. *To See the Dream*, published in 1958, details
nine months of grappling with stars, producers, scene
designers, and costumers in defense of her story and
characters. In the process, she offered a revealing look at
the behind-the-scenes creative process, Hollywood style.
A reviewer wrote that the reader who begins reading *To
See the Dream* with a mild curiosity about Hollywood
finished the book with an absorbing interest in the
author.

Her ninth book and third novel, *A Matter of Time*, is
contemporary in both time and outlook. The story of a
courageous woman dying of cancer who chooses death on
her own terms, it is based on Jessamyn's experience helping her well-loved sister Carmen end her life. This new
dimension in her writing astonished one reviewer, who referred to her previous reputation as a "nice lady who
writes nice novels." To which the author replied, "I'm not
really very nice, and some of my novels have not been very
nice."

A Matter of Time was, in Jessamyn's words, "about as
joyous as any tragedy can be." Critics termed it "moving
and real, an act of bravery." According to one reviewer,
"To celebrate life in the presence of death requires more
than craft. It demands inner conviction that assigns
priority to purposes beyond drawing characters or
chronicling events."

Much later, she wrote a nonfiction account of the same
experience that comprised the second half of the book *A
Woman Said Yes*. Reprinted in *Family Circle* magazine,
the account drew a record number of letters. About half

the mail was sympathetic and expressed admiration for the participants in this real-life drama. The other half declared vociferously that Jessamyn West deserved to roast in hell. "I may roast in hell," says Jessamyn, "but it's not going to be for sitting with Carmen during her last days."

A Woman Said Yes, of all the things she's written, is the book she's happiest with. "I wanted to praise my mother," she says. "I didn't appreciate her while I was growing up. She was too spunky and spicy, but now I have begun to understand the type of woman she was. And I wanted to praise my sister. When I finished writing it, and it was published, I thought, *O.K. I can die now. I don't want to.* As a matter of fact" — she smiles — "I try not to."

For a woman expected to succumb before she had written a word for publication, Jessamyn West has amassed an impressive collection of work. Her books number sixteen: *The Friendly Persuasion* (1945), *A Mirror for the Sky* (1948), *The Witch Diggers* (1951), *Cress Delahanty* (1953), *Love, Death and the Ladies' Drill Team* (1955), *To See the Dream* (1957), *Love is Not What You Think* (1959), *South of the Angels* (1960), *The Quaker Reader* (1962), *A Matter of Time* (1966), *Leafy Rivers* (1967), *The Chilkings* (1967), *Except for Me and Thee* (1969), A Companion to *The Friendly Persuasion* (1969), *Crimson Ramblers of the World, Farewell* (1970), *Hide and Seek* (1973), *The Secret Look* (1974), *The Massacre at Fall Creek* (1975), and *The Woman Said Yes* (1976).

The wide variety of forms she has used to express her creativity is amazing. Jessamyn has written science fiction, essays, poetry, short stories, novels, an opera libretto, profiles, and nonfiction articles for magazines, movie scripts, autobiography, memoirs, and personal journals (unpublished) by the dozens. She says her philosophy of

A publicity photo of Jessamyn taken in 1945
for her book The Friendly Persuasion

writing is the same one that puts her through the trauma of creating a new dish each time she entertains: failure is better than repetition.

Magazines sometimes ask her to write profiles of famous women. She's interviewed Jimmy Carter's faith-healing sister and assassin Lee Oswald's wife, Marina. She also wrote a piece on Pat Nixon, her cousin Richard's

*Jessamyn in 1946 with her first car; she bought it with
money earned from publication of* The Friendly Persuasion.

wife. After leaving the presidency, Nixon sent Jessamyn (a
Democrat) his book in which he wrote, "For my cousin
Jessamyn, who is the most noted writer of the Milhouse
clan, from the most notorious."

While she takes on various projects suggested to her by
magazine editors, fiction is her first love. She says she feels
imprisoned if she must stick to facts, that writers should
leave something to the imagination. She usually begins
with a character in a situation. She says that it would be
difficult to separate the person and what the person does
because his actions tend to define and illustrate him. By
identifying with somebody within the book, she is able to
report the events as if "they were on my pulses."

Jessamyn sees writing as a process of self-exploration.
For her, it is the ultimate way of examining who she is. By
immersing herself in her characters, she has discovered
what she would be like had she been a Quaker minister,
an Indiana farmer, or a woman dying of cancer. She has
never been able to write about someone who is totally
defeated. Her interest is in situations in which people
learn, in which life is used to some purpose.

One thing she has found in her lifelong struggle for self knowledge is that she has trouble portraying an evil person. Since she believes no one is a complete writer unless she can write about evil, she sees this inability as a distinct lack. She says, "If you are yourself evil, you understand how you became that way, and you forgive yourself. So no one in my books comes across as being truly very awful. I wonder what I would do if I were made to write about someone truly evil?"

Jessamyn's approach to the novel is of one whose pen, as one critic expressed it, is "dipped in love." She once wrote that hate can motivate writing "as explosive as a blow but it is utilitarian writing, put together not to reveal but to destroy."

Described by one reviewer as being almost hysterically alive, Jessamyn admits, "Perhaps I have been too easily pleased with life because I once thought I could not live long." Certainly she makes it clear she is not interested in life lived on any halfway basis. As a graduate of the terminal ward, she understands the preciousness of time. If you insist on thinking only of heaven, she warns, you'll someday regret missing the wonders of living on earth.

Jessamyn's idea of full living is to write. She admits that she is not an inspired writer, that the work is difficult. Often she's impatient with efforts that don't measure up to her image of what they should be, but there isn't anything she would rather do. She loves the physical act of writing words on a page and says she doesn't feel quite complete without a pen in her hand.

Retirement has never entered the mind of this vivacious seventy-seven-year-old woman. She wants to write until she dies. "A lot of people were winding up their writing when I was starting," she says. "I have the feeling I'd better write twenty years longer than most writers because most of them started twenty years earlier."

First, she says that she was an avid reader. A writer should make up his mind between writing and reading because she doesn't think there's time for both. Admittedly, she's never made up her mind. She's always surprised to hear of writers who ration themselves a limited time for reading each day. That would never work for her since she goes to sleep reading and wakes up reading. She still has the feeling that someday in a book she'll find the great treasure she's been looking for all her life.

"The trademark of a writer," she says, "is a love of words. People sometimes say that the most essential quality for a writer to have is a love of people, but if he loves people he should be a teacher, a nurse, or manage a massage parlor."

Although she's advised and taught a number of writers' conferences, Jessamyn questions their value for a would-be writer. Speeches are often entertaining, but she doubts whether anyone improves his writing skills by listening to them. Real learning and growth take place in writing and rewriting. Her major contribution, she feels, is in individual criticism of work already completed. By sharpening up a beginning or demonstrating where to tighten a story most effectively, she is best able to help aspiring writers.

Once having decided to write, a person should begin at once practicing the craft. "That's just what I didn't do," she says with exasperation. She still regrets those lost years and wishes she had had the courage to begin earlier "because there are things you can only say when you're young." As to why she put off doing what she was so perfectly suited for, she says she admired birds and flying, too, but thought it was for a different order of beings. Surely one didn't just pick up a pen and begin writing!

Jessamyn cites this lack of courage as her least favorite trait. She chastises herself for knowing and thinking things and not doing anything about them. She says, eyes blazing, "I don't stick my neck out. I take what comes to me. In my whole life situation of meeting people, of dealing with people, I haven't been courageous."

She guards her writing time jealously. Jessamyn writes reclining in bed, a habit carried over from her years recovering from tuberculosis. One benefit of writing in bed is that it is an effective way of coping with distractions. She says that once she gets up and puts on some decent clothing, she sees so many things that need to be done she's apt to get sidetracked.

The problem of other people intervening is not limited to housewives like herself. She says any writer has parents, friends, and acquaintances. When her mother and father visited, they would have liked to have spent all day with her, but she wanted to shut the door and immerse herself in her writing.

"People just don't think of writing seriously. If I had been going off to teach all day, it would have been different. They wouldn't interrupt your work if you were employed at a grocery store. That's considered serious business. It's because you work at home. People think they can interrupt writing," Jessamyn says with resignation.

Does she, raised in the days before the woman's movement, feel guilty taking time for her writing that could be spent with her husband? No, but she has felt guilt when she's neglected her work to entertain in her role as school man's wife. As for overshadowing her husband, this well-known writer laughs. "In Napa, California, I am the superintendent's wife. Most people aren't readers, anyway. If they are, they are probably afraid I'll put them in my next book."

Solitude has always excited her, especially when the opportunity for it must be stolen, as it must in most family

Jessamyn West (photo by Bill Gleasner)

situations. Even as a small child, Jessamyn remembers treasuring time alone. She claimed an old metal washtub as her own, only to find her two-year-old brother also found it irresistible. In spite of her warnings, he insisted on climbing into the private retreat to join her. She told him to leave, but he didn't listen, so she solved the problem by biting him. She admits it wasn't a nice way to have started her quest for solitude but that it worked. No one wanted to get in that tub with her again.

As an adult, she once lived by herself for three months in a travel trailer on a remote bank of the Colorado River.

Besides treasuring solitude in and for itself, she wanted to
have time and quiet for writing. The book resulting from
this interlude was *Hide and Seek*. In it she speaks of the
female writer's constantly guilty conscience. She says that
when a woman wants to be alone, she feels "wicked,
unloving, defying God and man alike," whereas "men, in
this instance (as in most), consider themselves on the side
of the Lord God."

Another handicap the female writer must overcome is
that often she's had a more restrictive existence. Men
have usually lived expansively, says Jessamyn, and have a
wide range of experiences from casual conversations at a
bar to fist fights and wars.

But Jessamyn is quite cognizant of the blessings of being a woman. How could she have written had she been a
man? She says she would have had to find some work that
didn't undermine her once-frail health. While the
woman's experience is limited, Jessamyn points out she
often has someone to support her, which leaves her free to
write.

The woman's movement fills her with "amazement, admiration, and wonderment." Her background is not
typical for a woman of her age partly because she hasn't
felt a lack of assertive female role models. For one thing,
she says, Quaker women were liberated from the beginning. They were preachers just as often as men were. It
was a commonly accepted practice for them to go into
prisons and read Scripture to the inmates. They also felt
free to go on missionary trips without their husbands.

Jessamyn says, "I would be the first one to scream if I
didn't get paid as much as a man. I think if you want an
abortion, you should have it." But she takes issue with
feminists who think we all should be operating very spe-
cifically as men and women. She says, "I prefer to operate
as a human being." But, male or female, she doesn't

think a career alone is enough. She feels there's a strong need to love another human being and that life is incomplete without that love.

She questions the way she was raised. A violin was purchased for her younger brother, she remembers, and she was to accompany him. In those days, girls were rarely given a solo. She says, "At the time, I was completely one with my mother in thinking Myron should play the solo and I should accompany. Later, looking back, I thought it was discriminating for the girl always to accompany the boy, who got the solo part."

Because she was the oldest, her mother made her play the role of man of the family. When some boys taught her brother bad words, she was sent to scold the offender. She feels it would have been better for her brother to have assumed the role of the younger boy's protector. Besides, all she got out of the encounter was a bloody nose!

"I was not only liberated," remembers Jessamyn, "I was doing what a boy should do. I thought I was better than boys. I could outrun a boy. I also thought the way to make boys like me was to be like one. So I tried to walk like a boy. What I figured out was that boys didn't bend their knees as much. Evidently, I did something strange, because when I went back to high school after I graduated, the principal said without hesitation, 'Hi there, Jessamyn.' When I asked him how he remembered me, he said, 'I'd never forget that walk.' "

She missed the stage common to many teenagers of hating her hair or her legs or any other part of her body, though she admits "breasts seemed, when they appeared, an unneeded excrescence." She thought of herself as transparent and considered her body good transportation. She could run faster than most boys. But she says she lived in what she felt and that there was too much feeling to leave much room for worrying about looks.

The upbringing of girls in her generation, she feels, was wrong in a good many ways, yet it did not keep her from having a strong sense of self. Mary Jessamyn West remembers vividly coming home from the library with an armload of books one starry evening and feeling compelled to say out loud, "You are M. J. West." That is how she signs her name to anything she considers important. Legally, socially, and conventionally, she's Mrs. H. M. McPherson. But, she says, the truth of the matter is she is Jessamyn West.

Jessamyn has written that barriers in female relationships have existed because of woman's predicament of being a second-class citizen in society. She had for so many years no life separate from a man, wrote West, that she never said anything about the fun and satisfaction she found in friendships with other women. But she is optimistic about the future. "It may be, as the monks saved learning during the Dark Ages," she says, "that women will be the ones to save friendship in an age of social sludge."

Jessamyn's liberated outlook does not preclude domesticity. She describes herself as a woman who likes to keep house. "Is there anything more beautiful," she asks, "than a room you cleaned yourself?" Cooking she sees as tedious small muscle work that she does not enjoy. Cooks cook for others, she says, while house cleaners tend to work for their own pleasure. She says bringing order to her home does for her soul what prayer does for other people. And it takes a lot less faith. "House ordering is my prayer," she says "and when I have finished, my prayer is answered. And bending, stooping, scrubbing, purifies my body as prayer doesn't."

Ms. West lives in a very neat book-lined house in Napa Valley, California, that she shares with her husband of fifty-six years, Max McPherson, and a variety of cats and

Jessamyn in her California home (photo by Bill Gleasner)

dogs. She has expressed her need to give and receive love in an article written some years ago titled "Love is Not What You Think," which was later published as a book. Clearly, she thrives on a balance of companionship and solitude.

As for herself, she warns, "If you like a book, maybe you'd better not meet the writer because she's only what's left over; most of her has gone into the books."

This exuberant woman, who swims nude, compares housework to a prayer, and travels with a trunkload of books, is obviously much, much more.

Phyllis A. Whitney

ALONE AT FIFTEEN! The possibility was disturbing. Phyllis pushed it out of her mind. Whatever happened, whatever was going to happen, she would have to be ready for it.

Her father had recently died. Now her mother discovered she, too, had cancer. What if she died? Phyllis had no brothers or sisters. Her only relatives lived half a world away in the United States of America. She felt powerless as her life seemed to be slipping out of control.

Her mother hid her grief in a flurry of plans. She was determined to get her daughter settled in America so Phyllis would not be left in the Orient without any family. Phyllis Whitney was born in Yokohama, Japan, and spent her childhood in Japan, China, and the Philippines. Her American parents, Charles and Lillian Whitney, intended to one day take their daughter "home" to the states, but her father had been busy in shipping and later in the hotel business. He could not have guessed the sad circumstances that prompted his wife and daughter to pack their lives into many trunks and suitcases as they prepared to leave Japan.

Phyllis at about age three

America was Phyllis Whitney's dream. Others said she had an exciting childhood, one that might have come from the pages of a romantic novel. Her "school bus" had once been a sedan chair carried up the mountain by strong Chinese men. But the lands of her youth seemed everyday life to her. Her idea of an "exotic" country was the United States. Conflicting emotions pulled her in different directions. Grief for her father and worry about

Phyllis when she lived in the Orient

her mother collided with the realization that she was finally going to America.

Her first years in the states passed quickly. No sooner had Phyllis become familiar with Berkeley, California, than they moved to San Antonio, Texas. She learned to be adaptable, to be at home wherever she was, but it was also a sad time. Helplessly, the seventeen-year-old watched her mother fight a losing battle. Before she died, Mrs. Whitney arranged for her daughter to live with an aunt in Chicago. Phyllis realized she would soon have to make her own way.

The loss of her parents left her feeling desolate. She felt less lonely when she was busy, so she immersed herself in school work and dancing. As a child, she had thought of herself as plain and unattractive until she began dancing lessons. When she caught the spirit of the music and moved gracefully through a series of difficult steps, she glowed. She felt beautiful.

While still in elementary school, she had announced that she wanted to be a ballerina. Her mother had gently reminded her that a dancer's life was very demanding, that it took years and years of practice. Not one to be discouraged by the threat of hard work, Phyllis devoted herself to improving her skills. A rigorous workout was a tonic she was to rely on throughout her life.

When she was in eighth grade, Phyllis had been encouraged to write by her missionary school teacher in Kuling, China. Her parents had been so proud of her efforts. She remembered how satisfying it had been to hear her mother read her stories aloud. Those days now seemed far away.

She continued to write but missed her appreciative audience. It was clear that her stories would have to get into print or they would never be read. Artists could always hang paintings in their homes. Pages of typewriting would look pretty funny plastered all over her bedroom walls. As editor of her high school annual, she found one way to get into print. She could publish her own work!

Without money for college, Phyllis took a job after finishing high school. She thought she might enjoy being a librarian but soon found routine filing work tedious in the Chicago Public Library's children's room. She was more suited to helping people with their purchases in the book section of a local department store and later at Womrath's bookstore.

In her spare moments, she began to work seriously at

the craft of writing. Her ballerina dream had faded quickly in the harsh light of reality. "For a long time," she says, "I thought I was going to dance professionally, but gradually I found I was a much better writer than I was a dancer. Besides, a dancer's life is so hard; few are able to make a living at it. At least writing could be done on the side while I was working to support myself. And it could be pursued anywhere."

Her job left little time for writing, but Phyllis learned how to create time. She wrote after work and on weekends when others were going to the movies.

With enthusiasm and determination only to guide her, she learned by trial and error. She made, she remembers, every mistake there was to make, but she learned one valuable lesson well. She never gave up, even when her stories came back again and again with printed rejection slips clipped to them. No matter how carefully worded, these slips always said, "No." She rewrote the stories, mailed them to another editor, and waited. Someday, she hoped, someone would think one good enough to print.

As the years went by, doubts grew. Finally, after three years, an editor typed a note on the bottom of a rejection slip. "Work on characterization," it said. "Your characters lack dimension." The same week she received another bit of proof that someone was at least reading her work. "Interesting," an editor wrote in heavy black ink, "but not right for our magazine. Try us again."

She dashed down to the nearby newsstand to buy a new stack of magazines. Early in her writing attempts, she had learned that it was hopeless to try to sell to the high-paying shiny periodicals known as "slicks." So she studied the ones called "pulps," which were printed on cheap pulp paper. There, if anywhere, she would have a chance.

"I write for these magazines," she explained as she paid for them at the stand. It was true, after all. She did write

for them even if they didn't buy her work. The man hand-
ing her the change looked unimpressed. "It seemed a bit
better to be writing for them," she later explained to her
bookstore friends, "than to be caught reading them." She
admits she was a snob and has learned better now. "A
craftsman must respect her market," she says. "This I
learned to do."

After four years of writing without a single sale, she decided to put forth one final effort and enter *Liberty* magazine's short-story contest. She had written a story that
had promise. Several editors had made encouraging
remarks in their letters of rejection. After having it returned for the seventeenth time, she read it over, pretending it was someone else's work. It had been out for three
months, so it was easy to think of it that way. The story's
flaws jumped out at her. She began again. The idea was
good, but the characters were wooden. Instead of talking,
they gave speeches. Phyllis studied books from the library
to learn how authors brought their characters to life. She
invented a new subplot, mercilessly cut out unnecessary
words, added motivation for her character's actions, and
gave the ending a new and satisfying twist. After much
pruning and polishing, she reread it out loud. It was
good. Not only good, it was the best work she had ever
done. With much hope, she mailed it to *Liberty*.

A few weeks later, she arrived at her apartment after a
hectic day at the store to find mail from *Liberty*, not a
large package with a rejected story but a slim first-class
letter. Her hopes soared as she tore at the envelope. Her
eyes flew down the page. "You are to be congratulated.
The judges ranked your story number eleven in our contest which drew hundreds of entries. Although you missed
qualifying for one of the ten prizes, we know you will be
pleased to have come so close. Your story will be returned
under separate cover. Thank you for entering our con-

test." It was signed by the editors of *Liberty* magazine.

Pleased? She felt only numbness. Her best effort had failed to get into print. It was simply not good enough. No one could have tried harder. No one could possibly have cared so much.

Later, much later, she would look back on that day as the lowest point in her writing career. Yet years of discouragement had trained her to be tough, to try again. Two weeks later, she was back at her desk. Within a month she sold her first story to the *Chicago Daily News*. Success, small as it was, had not come too soon.

The wonder of it stayed with her a long time. Someone had actually paid for her story. The byline read "Phyllis A. Whitney." She was a published writer.

But she was to learn that editors do not dole out checks to reward dedication and sacrifice. They buy the best material they can, and Phyllis was entering a very competitive marketplace. Even at the one-cent-a-word pulp magazines, her stories were just part of the "slush pile," as unsolicited manuscripts are called. They had to be better than any others in order to attract attention. Although she had learned a great deal during her four-year apprenticeship, there was still more to master. The fine tuning the pros gave their writing would be accomplished only through more practice.

In the next three years, she sold a grand total of four stories to pulp magazines and Sunday school papers. Phyllis had long ago stopped counting rejection slips. Each sale had been a personal victory, a dose of encouragement that sent her floating to her typewriter to try to recreate her success. Four stories in seven years! "That's how bad I was," she says, "and that's how much I wanted to be a writer." At that rate, she would have to live a long time in order to make a mark in the world of writing.

Today, as she holds her sixtieth book, she knows well

the cost. "Any success demands a price," she says, "and the time and effort and sometimes anguish a successful person gives to his work is that price. For me, the satisfactions have been worth it."

When Phyllis Whitney married in 1925, a year after graduating from high school, the idea of a woman pursuing her own interests was often questioned. Her neighbors assumed she would be happier mending socks than exploring her gift of creativity. When they learned she was paid only a few dollars a story, they wanted to know why she wasted her time on them. One suggested Phyllis might be better off learning to be a better cook and housekeeper.

The women's movement and the philosophy of exercising your own potential were years away, but the spirit that flamed them was alive in Phyllis. "I have always been out there doing my thing even though some people didn't approve of it," she says.

Domestic chores paled beside the thrill of seeing her stories in print. Her background had not been exactly traditional. In the Orient, she had lived mostly in hotels. Her greatest shock on arriving in America had come when a friend's mother asked her to wipe the dishes.

Phyllis's pregnancy seemed to give neighbors renewed hope for her domesticity. "There won't be any time for writing with a new baby," they warned. No time for writing? She'd written three hundred stories while holding a full-time job. How could a baby stop her? New ideas constantly sent her mind delving into a separate world populated by fascinating characters. Every story published strengthened her resolve to hone her skills.

Of her first marriage, Phyllis says, "It would have been better for my husband if I had been a domestic type of woman, but I wasn't that kind of person. My writing and my success, minor though they were at the time, were

Phyllis and her daughter Georgia when Georgia was fifteen

probably a threat. It was not his fault. We married too young. If two people grow in opposite directions, how can they stay together?

"At first my income was miniscule," she remembers, "but I had finally begun to sell some stories before I wrote my first book." After being turned down by two other firms, *A Place For Ann* was published in 1942 by Houghton Mifflin. This first book for young people convinced Phyllis to change the focus of her energy from short stories to books. Gradually, her writing caught on, and the money started to come in. An escape from an unhappy marriage was then possible.

The divorce in 1945 after nineteen years of marriage was painful. Her daughter Georgia was eleven, and it was sometimes difficult combining a career with being a mother. But Phyllis had learned the importance of daily writing. "I wrote right around her," she says. "She learned to respect my work and at the same time to entertain herself. We're very close now, though since she was not allowed to interfere during my working hours, there was some natural resentment when she was small. Nevertheless, she became a very good critic and still is. I began to read my books aloud to her when she was nine years old, though I was writing for teenagers. She would tell me frankly what she thought. Georgia went in a different direction when she grew up and is now an artist with three children of her own."

Phyllis's dedication to her work came as much from her desire to write as it did from her need for an income. She says, "It's necessary for every human being to be selfish some of the time. If you are completely unselfish, you are a nonentity and end up not doing anyone any good. Writing is what I wanted most to do."

A fifteen-year apprenticeship perfecting the short-story form gave Phyllis the strong foundation she needed to tackle larger projects. She says that the short story is the most difficult form of writing, that it provided the ideal training ground for her later work. Even though she turned out more than three hundred stories of mystery, romance, and suspense, she says she is not a natural short-story writer. For proof, she offers the fact that less than one hundred stories actually sold to magazines. The rest remained in her file, testimonials to her perseverance.

After four successful career books for girls, Phyllis yearned for a new challenge. When she suggested the black-white racial problem, her editor objected. "Don't write it," she said. "We won't take it." But Phyllis refused to be dictated to. Once again, she was ahead of her time. Civil rights legislation was years away when she decided the problem was too important to be ignored. "There was a good deal of intolerance on the part of Americans in the Orient toward the Eurasians," she remembered, "and it always made my mother indignant. I had the same disturbed feelings when I came to the states and found we

Americans could be intolerant toward some of our own citizens."

Willow Hill, her fourth book, was not easy to write. It went beyond the career books she had been doing into new and difficult territory. She wanted to be sure it was good enough to do justice to its theme. With great relief, she finally turned the finished manuscript over to Frederic Nelson Litten, a respected writing teacher at Northwestern University.

"Phyllis," he said when he handed it back, "you know better. You're on a soap box all the way through, preaching to your readers. You've got to bring your characters on stage and let them tell their own story."

His criticism devastated her. "I'm finished as a writer," she told herself. "It's just not worth it. I'll show him. I'll never write again, ever." Looking back, she sees her reaction "as that of someone very immature. Blaming him for my shortcomings as a writer was my own way of protecting myself. How foolish it was to think my quitting would harm anyone but myself."

Experience and maturity later enabled her to put the incident into perspective. But at the time the hurt went deep. However, during the entire six weeks that she "quit writing forever," she suspected he was right. Later, she attacked the problem head-on and rewrote the entire book. This time the characters came up with their own solutions. It worked. Fred Litten's diagnosis had been right on target. Learning to accept criticism from knowledgeable people was a great step in her professional growth and has been useful to her ever since.

Willow Hill, the story her editor had told her not to write, became a very successful book. Readers of all ages identified with its characters. One reviewer called it a "sensitive, realistic treatment of contemporary American life and youth—vitalized by the author's genuine concern with an important problem." *Willow Hill* was awarded a $3,500 prize in David McKay Company's *Youth Today* contest.

Bolstered by this success, Phyllis went on to delve into other controversial areas ranging from the story of a guide at the United Nations to the subject of migrant workers, from stepfamilies to the growing problem of divorce. By this time, she was becoming well known for her mysteries for young people. Books such as *Secret of the Emerald Star*, with a blind girl as one of the main characters, combined a serious problem with an entertaining suspense story. Most of these books are about teenagers trying to get to know and understand those of different races, religions, or just other members of their own family.

Experts warned repeatedly never to use a girl as a main character in a mystery. "Boys aren't interested in reading about girls," they told her. But Phyllis felt the story would be more believable if she could identify with her main character. Besides, she saw her heroines as active participants in quest of adventure, not just sitting in the kitchen listening to mama. Phyllis always wrote using a feminine viewpoint and developed a loyal following of both sexes. Now her fan mail from boys is as enthusiastic as the letters she receives from girls.

Looking back on these early struggles, Phyllis says, "A learning period must be allowed for any talent. The accidental success is unfortunate because the person who achieves it doesn't really know how it happened. This does not mean that it ever becomes easy, even with learning. There is always work involved and long hours and dedication to that work before a book is ready for publication."

Did she ever think that one day she'd be one of the best-selling authors in America? The idea shocks her. "I never *planned* to be successful. I never dreamed I'd be really successful. I just wanted to write well enough so somebody would read me! After my first book, I simply went on trying to be a little better each time, doing the best I could on each new book. Progress is made in a series of level stretches which can run along for some time before the next level up is reached. For a while, you think there isn't going to be any change, and suddenly you've moved up. You don't ever 'arrive.' You just keep traveling."

After a number of successful books for teenagers on social problems, Phyllis decided to try period stories. *Step to the Music* with a Civil War background is, in her opinion, one of her best teenage novels. When the editor of the People's Book Club suggested she try a book for adults, she reluctantly agreed. She was not at all sure she could do it. The result, *Quicksilver Pool*, proved she had underestimated her abilities. It was the first of a long series of successful romantic-suspense novels.

These tales are usually set in old mansions against an exotic background. Because locale is so important to the flavor of the intrigue, she combines her background research with a love of travel to get first-hand impressions.

"After I learn all I can about the location in the library, I travel, take extensive notes, and collect snapshots," she says. "I write from the viewpoint of a stranger coming into a new place. This way I'm able to look at everything through the eyes of an outsider who cannot possibly know as much about the place as someone who lives there. Then when the book is done, I always have it read by a local resident who can catch those mistakes it's impossible for a stranger to avoid. I want my background details to be accurate."

In the process of launching into the adult field, Phyllis met Patricia Schartle (now the wife of writer Anton Myrer), who was an editor with Appleton Press. Later, when this excellent editor became an agent, she offered to represent the author. She would sell her work, negotiate contracts, and handle business details so Phyllis could concentrate on writing. After working on a number of books together, Phyllis sent Pat Myrer a Valentine signed with the names of the heroines in her novels. It was more than just a joke. Phyllis says, "I identify with all those women I write about. There is always some of me in them. I may not have the hangups I give them, but I can understand and sympathize with them." Today, Mrs. Myrer is still the most trusted critic of Phyllis's work as well as a valued friend and confidant.

Phyllis's attitude toward money has remained unchanged over the years. Her needs are modest, but she enjoys knowing she can help her grandchildren through college and travel whenever she wants. While financial security is a source of satisfaction, she counsels new writers never to write just for money. "The only way for money to come," she says, "is to be doing the best job you can at what you really want to do. When you deliberately set out to write for money, you defeat yourself. Your eye is on the wrong ball."

Phyllis Whitney's second marriage in 1950 to Lovell Jahnke was very happy. He believed in her career, always encouraged her, and showed great pride in her accomplishments. They enjoyed traveling to foreign countries to research backgrounds for her books. After twenty-three years of marriage, Phyllis had to face the major loss of her husband to cancer. "But I'm a fighter," she says. "I vowed to make a new life, to be happy. He would be proud of the adjustment I've made." Wistfully, she adds, "I'd still like to show him some of the things I do."

Phyllis Whitney's small but comfortable home on Long Island, New York, suits her well. "Interviewers are often disappointed," she says, "because I don't live in a mansion like my heroines, but all the mansions I really care about are in my books. I've lived in them while I was writing them."

Her approach to critics' reviews of her books is philosophical. "I don't pay too much attention," she says. "You give one book to ten people, and you get ten different reactions. So I trust my agent, and when I've done the best I can, and she's offered the best criticism she could give me, then we let the chips fall where they may. Some people are going to like a book, some aren't."

At this point in her career, she has no plans to go on to different types of writing. "I've found the medium in which I'm happy," she says. "I like mystery novels. It's a difficult form to master because the plotting is so complicated; you have to juggle so many balls at the same time. I still have to be willing to revise. Writing is labor, but I enjoy revision." Not long ago she tackled the largest revision ever when she completely rewrote *The Golden Unicorn*, a book she describes as her toughest one yet. Fortunately, the anguish doesn't show in the final version.

In the early days, she used to write down her goal each morning, stating how many words she was aiming for. At the end of the day, she would record how many she had actually written. She no longer does that because she says, "I have learned to trust myself. You have to have confidence you can work it out. I know I can and that I will do whatever is necessary to make the book a success. I never allow myself to be be discouraged."

She says, "Young people write to me and say they think when they grow up they will become writers. Well, that isn't the way you do it. You have to want to write. You write because you can't help it. Then nothing can stop you. There will be more rejections than sales in the beginning. You have to be ready to take all that early discouragement. But first of all you must like to put words on paper."

As a writer who learned the hard way, Phyllis Whitney decided early in her career to share her knowledge and experience with aspiring writers. For a year, she taught writing classes at Northwestern University and later for eleven years at New York University. Her *Writing Juvenile Fiction*, a classic in its field, was succeeded by the even more complete *Writing Juvenile Stories and Novels*, which takes the mystery out of writing for publication. Beginners who correspond seeking advice are warned to take a job to support themselves since few writers are able to accomplish that for a long while. She reminds them that nothing is more important than setting aside a certain period each day to write. Inspiration is fine when it happens, but determination and making a habit of writing are far more important.

Lack of a formal education was no deterrent. In fact, Phyllis believes now it might have helped. "I certainly don't feel uneducated. I've had a very good education," she says. "In the beginning, I regretted not having been to college, but I was such a poor writer then that professors might have urged me to forget it. Had I majored in English and had my eye on the fine writing in the classics, which I couldn't possibly do, I might have been discouraged from trying."

"Working in bookstores gave me a good perspective. Customers would come in and ask, 'What's good that's new?' They didn't want to know what *I* thought was good but rather what *they* would enjoy reading. I learned in the beginning that everyone has a right to like different kinds of books, and I have never put down reading as a form of entertainment. My readers often turn to my books as an escape from dullness or unhappiness."

After all the effort, the satisfactions are sweet. Phyllis cherishes those precious moments all writers work for: hearing from her agent or editor that a new book is well done, receiving the first copy of her latest publication, seeing the new jacket for her next book, passing the Phyllis Whitney shelves in the library. Letters from all over the world (her books are published in twenty countries) testify that her writing continues to provide readers with a great deal of pleasure.

The rewards continue because Phyllis keeps on writing. Retiring has never occurred to her. "I couldn't stop writing," she says. "I couldn't live." At seventy-five, she's still at the typewriter each morning following a schedule that includes regular hours of work interrupted only by exercise and meal breaks. She describes herself as disgustingly methodical and organized, and one look at her orderly desk confirms this. Even her pencils are organized. Those placed point down in the mug need sharpening; those upright are ready for use.

Her exercise breaks are timed with a stopwatch. She dances and skips rope fifteen minutes at a stretch three times a day, usually in front of the television set, since she finds this type of exercise boring. She says, "At seventy-five, I've got to keep active. I have to counteract the effects of sitting at the typewriter all day."

This sparkly eyed, vibrant woman looks more than twenty years younger than she is. Where does she get her energy, her youthful appearance? She points to rows of books on nutrition. "I study how to be healthy by paying attention to my diet," she says. She shuns refined flour and sugar and adheres to natural foods and vitamin and mineral supplements according to her needs. She has been able to shed a number of serious ailments thought to be chronic in senior citizens. Her doctors listen to her theories because she is living proof of what sound nutrition and a positive attitude can do.

How would she have changed her life if she could? "I would change nothing," she says. "All the agonies, the

Phyllis holding the stone bull that inspired her book The Stone Bull
(photo by Bill Gleasner)

pain, the losses, have made me the way I am now. Those
are the things that temper and strengthen you and make
you a human being. I think I've come to a place where
I'm fairly well balanced, content, and able to enjoy my
life. Few people at my age are having as good a time as I
am."

More than twenty years ago, Phyllis wrote that writers stay young more successfully than other people do. "Perhaps it is because no one who has a keen and lively interest in life can really grow old," she said. "And when you are a writer, your senses never atrophy. The person who is ever interested is ever young."

This sprightly woman is certainly ever young.

Noted British and American Women Writers

A Brief Selected Chronology

1640   *APHRA BEHN*. Brit. (1640?-1689)
Probably the first woman in England to earn her living by writing plays, poems, and novels.

1752   *FANNY BURNEY*. Brit. (1752-1840)
First important woman novelist in England, wrote *Evelina* in 1778.

1753   *PHYLLIS WHEATLEY*. Amer. (1753?-1784)
First distinguished black poet in America.

1759   *MARY WOLLSTONECRAFT*. Brit. (1759-1797)
HER *Vindication of the Rights of Women* (1792) was America's first woman-suffrage book.

1764   *ANN RADCLIFFE*. Brit. (1764-1823)
Wrote supernatural novels.

1775   *JANE AUSTEN*. Brit. (1775-1817)
Author of *Pride and Prejudice* who has been called the "mother of the English nineteenth-century novel."

1783   *LADY MORGAN*. Brit. (1783-1859)
Wrote romantic versions of Irish life.

147

1787   *MARY RUSSELL MITFORD.* Brit. (1787–
       1855)
       Sketches of rural life, character, and scenery
       in nineteenth-century Britain.

1788   *SARAH HALE.* Amer. (1788–1879)
       An editor and early feminist writer whose
       poem "Mary Had a Little Lamb" became a
       classic.

1797   *MARY SHELLEY.* Brit. (1797–1851)
       Creator of *Frankenstein.* Not responsible for
       any of the sequels.

1802   *HARRIET MARTINEAU.* Brit. (1802–1876)
       Novelist and authority on economics.

1802   *LYDIA CHILD.* Amer. (1802–1880)
       In 1826 she edited the first American chil-
       dren's periodical, *The Juvenile Miscellany.*

1806   *ELIZABETH BARRETT BROWNING.* Brit.
       (1806–1861)
       Well-known poet who wrote *Sonnets from the
       Portuguese.*

1809   *FRANCES KEMBLE.* Brit. (1809–1893)
       Her *Journal of a Residence on a Georgian
       Plantation* provides a unique view of slavery.

1810   *ELIZABETH CLEGHORN GASKELL.* Brit.
       (1810–1865)
       Wrote about the industrial troubles of the
       1840's.

1810   *MARGARET FULLER.* Amer. (1810–1850)
       An outspoken critic and editor who started
       The Dial magazine.

1811   *HARRIET BEECHER STOWE.* Amer.
       (1811–1896)
       Her *Uncle Tom's Cabin* was one of the best-
       known antislavery books.

1815   *ELIZABETH CADY STANTON.* Amer.
(1815-1902)
A dedicated suffrage advocate. She and
Susan B. Anthony published *The Revolution,* a New York women's rights weekly.

1816   *CHARLOTTE BRONTË.* Brit. (1816-
1855)
Best known for her classic novel *Jane Eyre.*

1818   *EMILY BRONTË.* Brit. (1818-1848)
Considered the greatest of the Brontës.
Wuthering Heights is one of the most widely
read works of English fiction.

1819   *GEORGE ELIOT.* Brit. (1819-1850)
Mary Ann Evans received encouragement, as
well as her pseudonym, from her lover,
George Lewes. She wrote some of the greatest
novels in the English language, including
Middlemarch, The Mill on the Floss, and
Silas Marner.

1819   *JULIA WARD HOWE.* Amer. (1819-1910)
Poet, dramatist, and lecturer on woman suf-
frage who is best known for her lyrics to "The
Battle Hymn of the Republic."

1820   *SUSAN B. ANTHONY.* Amer. (1820-1906)
Reformer and advocate of women's rights
who helped compile the *History of Woman
Suffrage.*

1820   *ANNE BRONTË.* Brit. (1820-1849)
The first words of her first novel, "All the
histories contain instruction," sum up her
pragmatic approach.

1821   *MARY BAKER EDDY.* Amer. (1821-1910)
The founder of Christian Science who began
her religious work by writing.

1830   *EMILY DICKINSON.* Amer. (1830–1886)
Largely unpublished in her lifetime, she is one of America's best-known poets.

1830   *HELEN HUNT JACKSON.* Amer. (1830–1885)
Worked toward better treatment of U.S. Indians. *Ramona* fictionalized the plight of the Indian.

1830   *CHRISTINA ROSSETTI.* Brit. (1830–1894)
Wrote poems of fantasy for the young.

1831   *MARY MAPES DODGE.* Amer. (1831–1905)
Wrote *Hans Brinker* and was the first editor of *St. Nicholas Magazine* for children.

1831   *REBECCA HARDING DAVIS.* Amer. (1831–1910)
One of the earliest American realists, she wrote about slums, racial bias, and political corruption.

1832   *LOUISA MAY ALCOTT.* Amer. (1832–1880)
Wrote autobiographical novels that are now considered children's stories. Best known for *Little Women*.

1839   *OUIDA (MARIE LOUISE DE LA RAMÉE).* Brit. (1839–1908)
Her forty-five novels feature highly romanticized heroes.

1846   *KATE GREENAWAY.* Brit. (1846–1901)
Her children's book illustrations set the style for children's clothing in nineteenth-century England.

1849   *FRANCES HODGSON BURNETT.* Amer. (1849–1924)
Author of *Little Lord Fauntleroy* and *The Secret Garden*.

1849   **SARAH ORNE JEWETT.** Amer. (1849–1909)
Wrote short stories, novels, and poems of the Northeast.

1857   **FANNIE FARMER.** Amer. (1857–1915)
Wrote one of the first usable cookbooks.

1857   **GERTRUDE ATHERTON.** Amer. (1857–1948)
Wrote *The Conqueror* and other historical fiction.

1857   **IDA MINERVA TARBELL.** Amer. (1857–1944)
Feminist and first female muckraker whose articles forced the dissolution of the Standard Oil Company of New Jersey.

1859   **KATHERINE LEE BATES.** Amer. (1859–1929)
Wrote "America the Beautiful" after a trip to Pike's Peak.

1860   **JANE ADDAMS.** Amer. (1860–1935)
Nationally influential worker with the poor who wrote *Twenty Years at Hull House.*

1865   **EDITH WHARTON.** Amer. (1862–1937)
First American woman to receive two Pulitzer Prizes.

1865   **ELIZABETH COCHRAN SEAMAN.** Amer. (1865?–1922)
Newspaper writer who exposed political and social evils and wrote under the name "Nelly Bly."

1866   **BEATRIX POTTER.** Brit. (1866–1943)
Creator of *Peter Rabbit*, considered the first modern picture book.

1867   **LAURA INGALLS WILDER.** Amer. (1867–1957)
Her first novel was published at age sixty-

five. Best known for *Little House on the Prairie.*

1870   *MARY JOHNSTON.* Amer. (1870-1936)
Author of *To Have and To Hold* and other popular historical romances.

1873   *WILLA CATHER.* Amer. (1873-1947)
Best known for *My Antonia* and *Death Comes for the Archbishop.*

1874   *AMY LOWELL.* Amer. (1874-1925)
Poet, critic, biographer, and editor with a reputation for shocking conduct and cigar smoking.

1874   *GERTRUDE STEIN.* Amer. (1874-1946)
An unconventional American expatriate who controlled the social and literary scene in Paris.

1880   *HELEN KELLER.* Amer. (1880-1968)
Deaf and blind from infancy. Her *Story of My Life* has been an inspiration to thousands.

1882   *VIRGINIA WOOLF.* Brit. (1882-1941)
Experimented successfully with the form of the novel. A prolific writer who encouraged women writers to insist on a "room of one's own."

1887   *EDNA FERBER.* Amer. (1887-1968)
A keen observer of American life well known for her novels *Show Boat* and *Giant.*

1890   *KATHERINE ANN PORTER.* Amer. (1890-   )
Her novels treat characters in disharmony with their environment. Author of *Ship of Fools.*

1891   *AGATHA CHRISTIE.* Brit. (1891-1976)
Her mysteries have had global sales of more than 300 million.

1892   *PEARL S. BUCK*. Amer. (1892–1973)
        An American raised in China who wrote *The Good Earth*. First American woman to win a Nobel prize in literature.

1892   *EDNA ST. VINCENT MILLAY*. Amer. (1892–1950)
        Poet and dramatist whose sonnets gathered critical and popular acclaim.

1893   *FAITH BALDWIN*. Amer. (1893–   )
        Popular novelist who sold over 10 million copies of her books.

1893   *DOROTHY PARKER*. Amer. (1893–1967)
        A caustic wit, poet, and critic who won the O. Henry Prize for her story "Big Blonde."

1897   *ENID BLYTON*. Brit. (1897–1968)
        Wrote over four hundred adventure stories for children.

1900   *MARGARET MITCHELL*. Amer. (1900–1949)
        Wrote *Gone with the Wind*, best-selling story of the Civil War.

1901   *MARGARET MEAD*. Amer. (1900–1978)
        Her *Coming of Age in Samoa* made anthropology popular.

1902   *JESSAMYN WEST*. Amer. (1902–   )
        Sensitive writer of novels and short stories.

1903   *PHYLLIS WHITNEY*. Amer. (1903–   )
        Best-selling author of romantic suspense novels.

1903   *CLARE BOOTH LUCE*. Amer. (1903–   )
        Her careers as playwright and diplomat were highly political.

1904   *NANCY MITFORD*. Brit. (1904–1973)
        Wrote lighthearted, amusing novels.

1904   *AYN RAND*. Amer. (1904–   )
        A Russian-born American who is a strong de-

fender of capitalism and the individual in her sometimes biographical novels.

1905   *LILLIAN HELLMAN.* Amer. (1905-   )
Best known for her plays *The Children's Hour* and *The Little Foxes.*

1907   *RACHEL CARSON.* Amer. (1907-1964)
Her book *Silent Spring* was largely responsible for today's environmental movement.

1909   *EUDORA WELTY.* Amer. (1909-   )
Offbeat stories of the South.

1912   *MARY McCARTHY.* Amer. (1912-   )
Versatile writer who has written everything from novels to criticism.

1914   *ANAIS NIN.* Amer. (1914-1977)
A dancer whose books were based on her diary started at age ten.

1915   *CAROLINE BIRD.* Amer. (1915-   )
Feminist who wrote *Born Female* in 1968.

1917   *GWENDOLYN BROOKS.* Amer. (1917-   )
Pulitzer Prize winner who published her first poem at age 13.

1917   *CARSON McCULLERS.* Amer. (1917-1967)
Novelist and playwright who examined the individual's search for love and happiness.

1919   *DORIS LESSING.* Brit. (1919-   )
Prolific novelist, short-story writer, poet, and playwright. *The Golden Notebook* is considered her masterpiece.

1921   *BETTY FRIEDAN.* Amer. (1921-   )
Her best-selling *The Feminine Mystique* challenged the prevailing idea that all women were happiest as homemakers.

1925   *FLANNERY O'CONNOR.* Amer. (1925-1965)
Wrote somber and grotesque stories on traditional Southern themes.

1927   *ERMA BOMBECK.* Amer. (1927–   )
Syndicated columnist and author of best-selling books of humor.

1928   *ANNE SEXTON.* Amer. (1928–1974)
Pulitzer Prize-winning poet.

1929   *MAYA ANGELOU.* Amer. (1929–   )
The first black woman to direct a Hollywood film, the movie version of her autobiography *I Know Why the Caged Bird Sings.*

1930   *LORRAINE HANSBERRY.* Amer. (1930–1965)
Author of *A Raisin in the Sun,* an honest, humorous look at big-city life of American blacks.

1932   *SYLVIA PLATH.* Amer. (1932–1963)
A sensitive poet, author of autobiographical novel *The Bell Jar.*

1934   *JOAN DIDION.* Amer. (1934–   )
Writer of intensely personal journalism and fiction.

1934   *KATE MILLETT.* Amer. (1934–   )
Artist, political activist, and author of *Sexual Politics.*

1934   *GLORIA STEINEM.* Amer. (1934–   )
Journalist, editor, active feminist, and co-founder of *Ms.* magazine.

1938   *JUDY BLUME.* Amer. (1938–   )
Best-selling author of juvenile fiction.

1938   *JOYCE CAROL OATES.* Amer. (1938–   )
Prolific novelist, short-story writer, critic, and essayist.

1942   *ERICA JONG.* Amer. (1942–   )
Author of *Fear of Flying,* feminist.

1943   *NIKKI GIOVANNI.* Amer. (1943–   )
Talented black poet.

Sources

Blume, Judy, *Wifey.* New York: G. P. Putnam's Sons, 1978.

Battelle, Phyllis. "The Real Erma Bombeck," *Good Housekeeping Magazine*, April, 1978.

Bombeck, Erma. "Do You Work or Are You Just a Housewife," *Ladies Home Journal*, February, 1978.

————. "How I Made It To the Top," *Ladies Home Journal*, October, 1978.

Doty, Carolyn. "Jessamyn West: The Art of Fiction LXVII," *Paris Review*, Vol. 70, Spring, 1977.

Dunn, Betty. "Socrates of the Ironing Board," *Life Magazine*, May, 1971.

Kessler, Judy. "Erma Bombeck, 'One Housewife's Boffo Woswell,' Finds Life is Anything but the Pits," *People Magazine*, May 22, 1978.

Emerson, William A., Jr. "Erma Bombeck Boasts: 'I Still Make the Beds and Scrub the Johns,'" *Today's Health*, December, 1974.

Goulianos, Joan, ed. *By A Woman Writt: Literature from Six Centuries By and About Women.* Indianapolis: Bobbs Merrill Company, Inc., 1973.

Graham, Lee. "An Interview With Jessamyn West," *Writer's Digest*, May, 1967.

Hutchens, John K. "Jessamyn West," *Herald Tribune Book Review Section*, February 18, 1951.

157

Maynard, Joyce. "Coming of Age with Judy Blume," *New York Times Magazine,* December 3, 1978.

Mitgang, Herbert. "Behind the Best Sellers," *New York Times Book Review,* April 23, 1978.

Moers, Ellen. *Literary Women, The Great Writers.* New York: Doubleday & Co., 1977.

Olsen, Tillie. *Silences.* New York: Delacorte Press/Seymour Lawrence, 1965.

People Magazine. "The 'Jacqueline Susann of Kids' Books,' Judy Blume, Grows Up With an Adult Novel," October 16, 1978.

Publishers Weekly. "Authors and Editors," April 28, 1969.

Saunders, Paula C. "Judy Blume as Herself," *Writers Digest,* February, 1979.

Shah, Diane K. "The $500,000 Housewife," *Newsweek Magazine,* January 2, 1978.

Shivers, Alfred S. *Jessamyn West.* Boston: Twayne Publishers, a Division of G. K. Hall and Co., 1972.

Showalter, Elaine. *A Literature of Their Own: British Novelists from Bronte to Lessing.* Princeton, N. J.: Princeton University Press, 1977.

Time Magazine. "Up the Wall with Erma," April 13, 1970.

West, Jessamyn. "Friendship Between Women," *Holiday Magazine,* March, 1964.

———. "Getting Personal," *PTA Magazine,* September, 1968.

———. *Hide and Seek.* New York: Harcourt, Brace, Jovanovich, 1973.

————. "Secret of the Masters," *Saturday Review,* September 21, 1957.

————. *A Woman Said Yes.* New York: Harcourt, Brace, Jovanovich, 1976.